MADE FOR A PURPOSE

MADE FOR A PURPOSE

LESSONS FROM MY SHEEPDOGS

DEBBIE L. COLE

XULON PRESS

Xulon Press
2301 Lucien Way #415
Maitland, FL 32751
407.339.4217
www.xulonpress.com

Unless otherwise indicated, Scripture quotations taken from the Holy Bible, New International Version (NIV). Copyright © 1973, 1978, 1984, 2011 by Biblica, Inc.™. Used by permission. All rights reserved.

Scripture quotations taken from the English Standard Version (ESV). Copyright © 2001 by Crossway, a publishing ministry of Good News Publishers. Used by permission. All rights reserved.

Printed in the United States of America.

ISBN-13: 978-1-66283-262-8
Ebook: 978-1-66283-263-5

ACKNOWLEDGEMENTS

Debbie wishes to acknowledge the following people:

Everett Hysten, a Bible scholar who has served the Lord as both a minister and elder for the church, for proof-reading and editing for scriptural accuracy and context of the Bible passages included. His review and edits for both *I Am A Sheep?!?!* and *Made For A Purpose* have been invaluable to my writing.

Nancy Simpson, proofreader and original editor before the manuscripts were submitted for both *I Am A Sheep?!?!* and *Made For A Purpose.*

Judy Davis, reader and proofreader of the original *I Am A Sheep?!?!* manuscript before it was submitted to the publisher.

Donnie Bonine, proofreader and editor before the *Made For A Purpose* manuscript was submitted.

Cara Eckman, photographer, for my author photo.

Beth Edwards Photography for the photo of the Fisher grandkids, the last photo before the glossary.

Professional handlers and sheepdog trainers of Texas who welcomed me, encouraged me, and taught me how to compete in sheep dog trials.

Kip, my husband, for all his encouragement and support of my writing.

DEDICATION

I dedicate this book to my daughters, Krystal Fisher and Valerie Roberts. My precious girls have become great mothers, making spiritual training and growth a priority in their homes. They have allowed me to share time with the grandchildren out in the pasture with the sheep. I could not be prouder of the godly women they have become. They are real blessings to me, to Kip, and to their families.

CONTENTS

INTRODUCTION

In 2010, I was blessed with a puppy who I named "Tux." Tux is an Auggie, a cross between two herding breeds, Welsh Pembroke Corgi and Australian Shepherd. The corgi breed was developed to herd cattle, while the Australian Shepherd is to herd sheep. In October of that year, Tux (nine mos.) and I went to the Corgi festival in Buda, Texas. Much to my delight, Tux passed an AKC sheepherding test with flying colors! With that successful test, I began looking for a place to train and herd sheep. I met several sheep dog handlers (*person controlling/training the dog*) who compete in sheep dog trials (SDT).

I bought my first border collie, Junebug, in January of 2012; she was already trained to herd sheep and follow commands from a handler. Rascal, another border collie, was added to my pack in 2015. She had started her training, but had much to learn before she was ready to compete in a sheep dog trial. As I was learning about sheep, and about myself and the Good Shepherd (our Lord, God), the dogs became an integral part of that learning process.

All three of those dogs were made for a purpose, which is to herd livestock, sheep in particular; yet they respond very differently to the master and to herding work. We too are made for a purpose by our Master and Good Shepherd, God Himself. I've written this book with lessons I've learned from sheepherding dogs. I pray their stories will bless and encourage you to fulfill our Master's purpose(s) in your life.

CHAPTER 1:
MADE FOR A PURPOSE

In the Beginning

We all know God created us and has a plan for our lives. But do we believe it deep down in our souls, to the point that we find our God-given purpose and pursue it wholeheartedly? It is not enough to know of God and believe He exists; we need to truly know Him and to have a relationship with Him, which requires time and effort on our part. It's not just so we can tick off the boxes. No, we need to truly come to know His character; to understand we need to walk with and follow Him with a desire in our hearts for a deeper relationship. In the sheep fields with my dogs, God spoke to my heart, not in audible words but by watching the sheep and the dogs – feeling convicted when I see myself in their actions as I serve Him.

God laid out His plan from the beginning, as we read in Genesis 1:26-27: "Then God said, 'Let us make man in our image, in our likeness' … So God created man in His own image, in the image of God he created him; male and female he created them" (NIV).

King David was inspired to give us more detail in Psalm 139: "For you created my inmost being; you knit me together in my mother's womb. I praise you because I am fearfully and wonderfully made; your works are wonderful, I know that full well. ...All the days ordained for me were written in your book before one of them came to be" (Ps. 139:13-14, 16 NIV).

Paul explains further in Ephesians 1:11-12: "In him we were also chosen, having been predestined according to the plan of him who works out everything in conformity with the **purpose** of his will, in order that we, who were the first to hope in Christ, might be for the praise of his glory" (NIV).

But sometimes we are a little uncertain in terms of His gifts and the purposes we were individually created to fulfill; at least I have been. In the sheep field, God, knowing I am a visual learner, used my sheepdogs to reveal His answer.

God has indeed gifted each one of us for His purposes, as written in the following Scripture verses: 1) "Many are the plans in a man's heart, but it is the **LORD'S purpose** that prevails" (Prov. 19:21 NIV). 2) "Each one should use whatever gift he has received to serve others, faithfully administering God's grace in its various forms" (I Pet. 4:10 NIV). 3) "For God's gifts and His call are irrevocable" (Rom. 11:29 NIV).

Since His gifts are irrevocable, we need to figure out what they are! Sometimes I've felt called to do something or felt God laid it on my heart to serve in other ways, but I was at a loss as to how. Growing up in the church, I always heard it said, "Ask God and He will show you." That statement is built on two premises: That I will indeed ask Him and that I will be looking for His answer. Both require me to be still and alert at all times.

LESSON 1

Be <u>obedient</u> to the Master; live to <u>serve</u>.

Origin of Border Collies

The border collie gets its name because the breed was developed on the border of Scotland and England in Northumberland. The sole purpose of the breed was to herd livestock, sheep in particular.

Today's herding lines of border collies are all descendants of Old Hemp, (1893-1901) an intelligent, quiet working dog used by many shepherds of the area because he had the reputation of being the best herding dog.

Good herding dogs work quietly and are kind to the sheep. They make every effort to move the sheep where the shepherd wants them, using their "eye" to guide (a focused stare at individual sheep or the flock as a whole). They use their speed to catch them and their proximity to the sheep to cover the draw, (the direction sheep want to go), and to encourage them toward the direction the shepherd wants. I must admit I cringe every time I hear someone talk about sheep-herding dogs in Bible studies because dogs are often given a bad rap. The sheep that respond and move as the dog guides them will never face a bite, but those that challenge the dog or charge it will experience a bite. The bite allowed in that instance by the shepherd or handler is often referred to as a "pop on the nose." The dog will snap in the air close enough to the sheep to brush the nose with its teeth, like a quick clamp and release. It must be understood that the dog has a specific purpose – go get the sheep and bring them to the shepherd, or get them into a pen or trailer. A dog cannot let a challenge, especially a charge, go without consequence; otherwise, the sheep will determine the dog has no power and refuse to submit. If a sheep is left behind because the dog does not convince the sheep to move, it becomes vulnerable to predators. Sheepdogs that simply grip or bite the sheep without provocation are disqualified in sheep dog trials and not looked on favorably by the shepherd.

We know from reading the book of Job that Old Hemp was not the first sheepdog in existence by any means, but he was made for a specific purpose. Job talks about his sheepdogs with pride, saying in Job 30:1, "But now they mock me, men younger than I, whose fathers I would have disdained to put with **my sheep dogs**" (NIV). The English Standard Version, Hebrew-Greek Key Word Study Bible states it differently but the tone is the same: "But now they laugh at me, men who are younger than I, whose fathers I would have disdained to set with the **dogs of my flock.**"

Shepherds agree that the border collie is indeed the most adept breed for herding, with their intelligence and stock sense. They are reported to be the most intelligent, athletic, and energetic breed of dogs, with no comparison to any other breed in terms of obedience. They live to serve, and that should be said about all Christians as well.

CHAPTER 2:
SHEEP DOG TRIALS

A sheep dog trial (SDT) is a herding dog competition of moving sheep through a preset course to win or place, resulting in points, which qualifies the dog for subsequent competitions and cash prizes. As humans, we also want to know who is best, who has the best; mine is better than yours. So, is it any wonder that SDTs developed along with herding dogs? The original premise of the trial was to have the course include obstacles and skills that are required by a good herding dog working the sheep on a farm. The main difference between a chore dog on the sheep farm and a competitive dog in sheep dog trials is the precision required to complete the task and the time it takes to get the job done.

For the sake of the reader who may be unfamiliar about sheepherding and sheep dog trials, let me share with you some terminology used that will be repeated throughout the book. It should be noted that the drawings are to give the reader a visual image of the SDT components. The exact placement of the dog or handler is relative to the position of the sheep and will vary in response to the sheep's reactions.

Terminology

Handler: A sheep-herding dog owner who uses a set of commands or whistles to direct the dog in gathering and driving sheep on a course for competition, or to do chores on the sheep farm.

God, Himself, does the same with us, "A man's steps are directed by the LORD. How then can anyone understand his own way?" (Prov. 20:24 NIV). Another good passage about God's direction for us: "I know, O Lord, that a man's life is not his own; it is not for man to direct his steps" (Jer. 10:23 NIV).

Run: A dog's turn to compete in the sheep dog trial.

The Post: Starting point of the dog's run, in competition; it is where the handler stands throughout the run until the sheep are to be penned or shed. If a handler leaves the post before the designated point the judge has determined, the judge lists it as RT, meaning the handler has chosen to retire *or quit*. No points are awarded when the handler retires.

Outrun: The dog leaves the handler at the post and runs out to gather the sheep in a wide arc until it comes in behind the sheep to move them. The arc needs to be wide enough to prevent scattering the sheep or sending them running before the dog lifts.

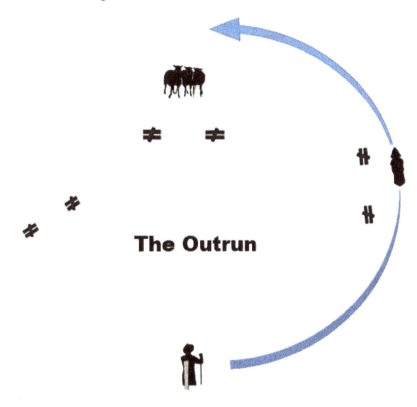

The Outrun

Lift: The dog moves the sheep from the position they were set out at the top of the field. A lift should be calm and quiet, with the sheep moving together in the direction of the post.

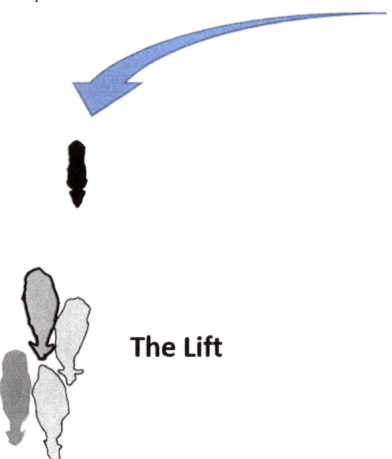

The Lift

Fetch: The dog brings the sheep from the set-out point to the handler at the post. There are fence panels set up between the post and the set-out; the dog is required to herd the sheep through the panels and in a straight line from the lift to the handler. Once the sheep are beside the handler at the post, the dog is to move the sheep around the post in a calm manner.

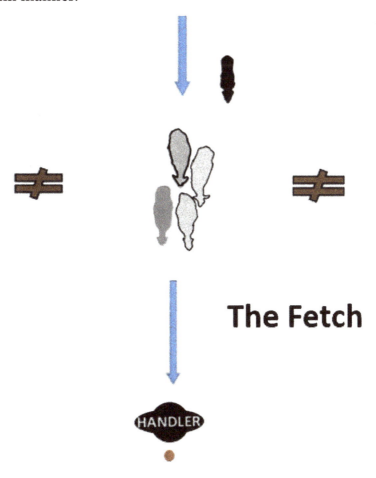

The Fetch

Rounding
the
Post

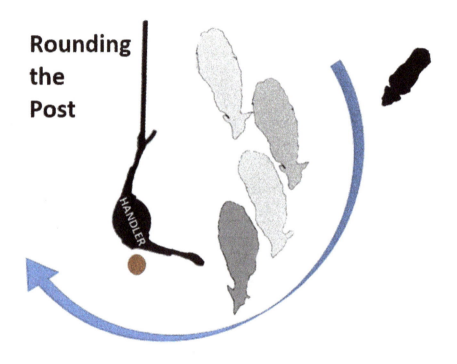

Drive: Fence panels are set up either to the right or the left of the post at a distance determined by the level of the dog in the competition. The dog is to drive or push the sheep away from the handler's post in a straight line and move the sheep through the panels. Once through, the dog is to turn the sheep toward the cross-drive panels.

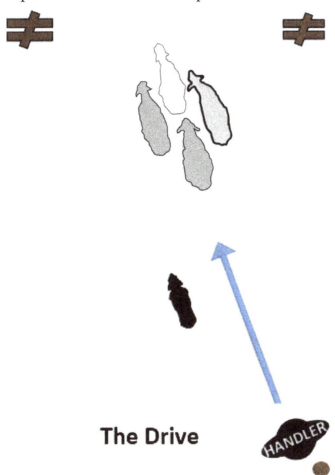

The Drive

Cross Drive: This is a distance across the width of the trial field. The dog is to drive the sheep calmly across the field in a straight line and move them through the panels on the other side of the field. He then turns the sheep toward either the shed ring or the pen, as directed by the handler.

The Cross Drive

Shed: The handler and the dog working together separate out sheep from the group and hold them separate until the judge acknowledges the shed. There is a ring marked on the course in some fashion, and the sheep must remain in the ring until the shed is complete. The judge will determine which sheep are to be shed, and points are given only if the specified sheep have been shed.

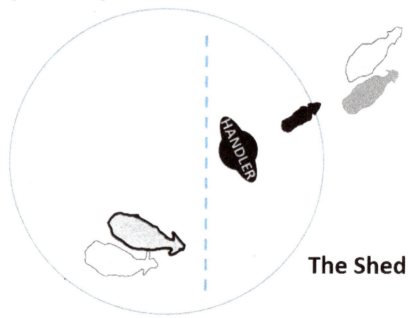

The Shed

Pen: A pen is set up on the course on either side of the post at a distance from the post. The handler will open the gate and hold onto a rope on the end of the gate. Together, the dog and the handler move the sheep into the pen and the handler closes the gate.

The Pen

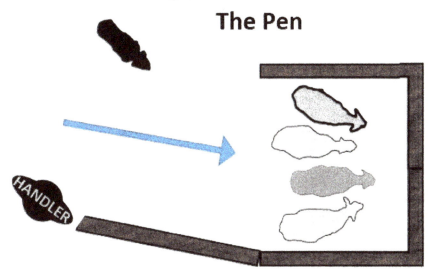

Gripping: That is biting the sheep with no provocation. The dog is immediately disqualified, and the handler must get their dog and leave the field.

Judging: The trial judge will determine the amount of time necessary to complete the course appropriately and will set a time limit for each run in the class. The judge is normally positioned up high enough to easily see if the lines are straight, if the sheep went through the panels, or if there is a grip. Each component has points assigned to it, and the judge will deduct points when the dog fails to meet the criteria as explained on the previous pages.

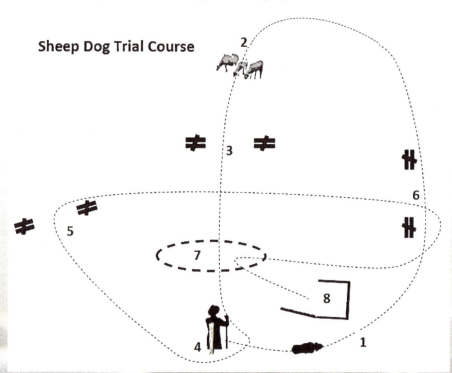

Sheep Dog Trial Course

CHAPTER 3:

TUX

My first introduction to sheep up close and personal took place at the Corgi Festival in Buda, Texas in October of 2010. When I decided to attend with a friend, also a corgi owner, I registered Tux for the AKC herding instinct test and for the Canine Good Citizenship (CGC) test. I bought Tux at eight weeks from a breeder in Oklahoma, and we started obedience training right away. We did the puppy class, the intermediate class, and the advanced class together. For the most part, he was obedient; however, corgis are known for their stubborn streak, and he certainly has one. *He is the queen's dog, but he is stuck with me.*

When we did the classes, he made me proud because although he is quite social, he was eager to please. But from the beginning, there were two things he fought me on: heeling (*walking right at my heel with his head even with my leg*) and not jumping on people. To this day, he insists that he must have his head in front of me when walking. When I am walking all three dogs, he refuses to be the dog at the back. Everyone who comes to visit, he still jumps up to meet.

At the Corgi Festival, we underwent the Canine Good Citizenship (CGC) test first. The CGC test judges the dog on ten obedience behaviors. Tux passed seven out of ten. To my dismay, he flat out refused to lie down when I gave him the command. In fact, he looked away from me, as if to say I am not doing it. I gave the command three times, and he refused each time. The tester said it was open defiance. *How embarrassing!* Next, it was our turn to do the herding instinct test. The tester had me join her in the round pen with Tux and the sheep. I had no clue what I was doing, but I did see Tux respond to the tester to change direction and he did respond to my recall. He passed the herding test and the tester told me we need to get training because of his natural ability to herd.

From October to December of 2010, I tried to make contact with a herding trainer, but to no avail. In December, I was invited to a club meeting for the local stock dog herding club. There I met a handler named Jewel, and she met Tux; we were invited to come to her place in January and learn sheepherding, where we went about every Saturday for six months. Tux learned to lie down and wait for a command to move toward the sheep. He learned flank directions, *Come by* (clockwise) and *Away to me* (counterclockwise), and the recall command, *That'll do here.* Jewel was delighted with his work and told me he was doing great. I could not see it, and I never really knew what I was doing. Jewel included me when she worked her lambs and sheep, banding, tagging, and giving vaccines, so I was getting hands-on practice working with sheep, but I was still green.

Jewel introduced me to a professional herding dog trainer and handler in the summer of 2011, to which I started taking lessons right away. The first time we met the trainer, it was quite the day. Jewel and the other handlers were there taking lessons with their dogs too. The big pasture where we were had a big shade tree in the middle of the property where we waited our turn. Tux was so excited, so I was working hard to hold his leash. Jewel suggested I put him on one of the tie-outs on the tree. I did that, but all of a sudden Tux broke free and made a beeline for the sheep (lambs actually). I was running down the field after him, yelling the recall command and he was ignoring me.

The next thing I knew the trainer was between Tux and the sheep, and her posture and voice he could not ignore. He laid down immediately. Whew! I was afraid there was going to be a catastrophe, but thankfully the trainer was fast and could growl a command that demanded attention. I was so embarrassed; the tie-out clip was old and a bit rusty, so it did not stay closed and that's how Tux got loose.

When it was our turn, the trainer led Tux and me up to a round pen with sheep that were *dog broke* (used to herding dogs) and not as reactive as the lambs down below. After the fiasco that had happened in the big pasture, I was afraid of how Tux would react. But like I said, the trainer knows dogs. She told me that I needed to learn to lower my voice, so it sounded firm and meant business rather than high-pitched meaning play time. (My voice always gets higher when I get excited or nervous, and so, to Tux, it sounded like puppy squeals and play time). In all the obedience classes, the tone of my voice was never mentioned, but now I had a plan to gain control and respect from Tux. I told Tux to *lie down* on one side of the pen and then walked away to join the trainer behind the sheep. He stayed in the *lie down* position until I gave him the next command. Hallelujah!

The first lesson taught me what to do with my crook to signal to the dog the command I am giving. Then, as the trainer told me the commands, she also took hold of my arm to guide me in the round pen. What an eye-opener! For the first time in months, I realized where I was supposed to be in relation to the dog and the sheep. Now I could see what the dog needed to do in relation to my position and the sheep. Soon I was able to practice in the round pen with the sheep while the trainer watched. As we learned each skill, Tux and I both grew in our confidence to move the sheep.

One thing the trainer suggested to me was to practice moving the sheep by myself, to pay attention to which way the sheep moved in response to my movements. I did that and what a difference it made in my ability to react, to predict, and to recognize how my position and the dog's position affected the movement of the sheep. The more practice I had on my own with the sheep, the more confident and adept I became at anticipating their movements and my timing in giving Tux commands.

I remember the day Tux and I graduated out of the round pen and into a small pasture for our lessons. It was a great day, and with more distance between the sheep and the post where I stood, I had more time to think and correct the dog's position in relation to the sheep. Soon, the day came when we were in the big pasture and the outruns (*distance from me to the sheep, the dog running in an arc*) were substantially greater. Tux and his short, little legs could run a wide arc either direction, clockwise or counterclockwise, and gather the sheep to me. He could drive them through the panels following my voice commands. One day, the resident horse was standing close to the arc Tux would be running for the outrun. I noticed Tux look at the horse and was afraid he might get distracted and get himself into-trouble, but he did not.

Working with the professional trainer, I began to learn the techniques for sheepherding. I learned how to handle and work Tux, along with the commands and skills necessary to be a competitive handler. Tux was very receptive in the beginning and eager to please, but as his confidence grew in his ability to herd the sheep, he became less obedient and more stubborn about who was in control. He could easily gather the sheep with a 175-yard outrun and bring them to me, and drive them through the panels on my command.

Open Defiance

Tux grew in his knowledge and confidence in his ability to move the sheep toward me or away from me, depending on the command I gave. But one day, he decided he would rather do his own thing and move the sheep where he wanted. In November 2011, we were taking a lesson and Tux, rather than gather the sheep to me, decided he would take them somewhere else. I repeated my commands and he ignored me. I went racing down the field to get between him and the sheep, to take the sheep away from him. It was not until I got close enough to grab him that he decided to obey me.

From that time on, anytime he was some distance from me, he would defy me and ignore my commands. I found myself running down the field again and again, lesson after lesson. It was so frustrating and became clear he was no longer a team player. And if I wanted to compete success-fully in this sport and do so in a manner that was safe and respectful of the sheep, I needed another partner.

The trainer suggested I may want to get another dog, and she had just the one. The trainer introduced me to Junebug, a border collie: she was already trained, ready to compete, and very eager for the opportunity. The trainer suggested I give her a try. I was so frustrated with Tux so, eagerly, I said yes. She brought Junebug out and we met for the first time. She is a black border collie with a little bit of white and some brown on her feet. The first time we met, she obeyed every command, brought the sheep right to my feet, drove them through the panels, and helped me pen them successfully. I walked her over to the post (starting position) and gave her the command for an outrun. She took off like lightning in a beautiful arc, coming in quiet and slow to lift (start moving) the sheep toward me. She brought them right to my feet, fol-lowed my direction in circling them around the post, and drove them through the drive panels, then straight across to the cross-drive panels and back to me at the pen. Together, we walked them in the pen. It was fabulous! She listened to me and knew what to do, and we worked great together the first time we tried. Wow! Finally, I felt what it was like to just pay attention to my job in guiding the dog where I need to and working as a team rather than fighting to be in control of the dog.

Consequence of Disobedience

Over the next few weeks, I thought about how thrilling it was working as a team and recognized that Tux was not a team player. I bought Junebug in January of 2012, so Tux was benched in terms of sheepherding and Junebug became my new best friend. I still have Tux and love him, but Junebug became my go-to dog for herding sheep.

I have thought a lot about the difference between Tux and Junebug. Both were bred for herding, but only one would listen to the master in the fields. It made me think about my relationship to the Father. I too was created for a purpose. I am to obey His will and follow Him, denying myself and seeking Him first. When I look back on my life, there are too many times that I, like Tux, ignored the voice of the Master. I was too busy running ahead, doing my own thing. When I scolded Tux, he would put his ears back and hang his head, but once we went out on the field again, he would disobey over and over. It was like he was saying, "I know she is going to yell at me, and I will be in trouble, but then she'll forget about it and everything will be fine again." There is a saying that it is better to ask forgiveness than to ask permission. How flawed that is, and yet we have the audacity to repeatedly defy God's will! Tux's behavior was so frustrating and infuriating to me; how dare he! Then I felt convicted in my soul, to where indeed, how dare I defy my Lord and Master. Worse, I have found myself in trouble for the same kind of disobedient behavior over and over again that I scolded Tux on.

In my case, I was not replaced like Tux but I did face consequences for my actions. I am sure God had to use other obedient servants to do the work He had called me to do or to clean up my mess. Just like Mordecai told Esther in Esther 4:14 (NIV): "For if you remain silent at this time, relief and deliverance for the Jews will arise from another place, but you and your father's family will perish. And who knows but that you have come to royal position for such a time as this?" God's will, will be done regardless! We can submit and obey and be used for His purpose, or He will use someone else in our place. I don't know about you, but I do not want to lose the opportunity to serve the Master because of my ego and selfish behavior.

I am ashamed when I think of how arrogant I have been in relation to the Master. When I think about how frustrated I was with Tux; how tired I got of running down the field after him to demand that he follow or he would lose his sheep. It makes me cringe knowing the frustration that I have also caused God by my own willful disobedience. I would have given up on me and not given me another chance, just like I took away Tux's opportunity to ever herd sheep again. Thankfully, our God is forgiving, patient, and long-suffering. He gives us opportunities to redeem ourselves and serve Him despite our sinful nature.

When I go ranch or farm sitting to take care of another's sheep, Tux is left behind and only Junebug and my other dog Rascal (the girls) get to go. Kip, my husband, says whenever the girls and I go away, Tux mopes about the house looking so sad, like he lost his best friend. At times, I have realized as I look back on my life, there were opportunities for service that I missed because I was too busy doing things my way. That makes me sad because I know I disappointed the Master and lost a precious opportunity to serve God like Tux did.

Some breeds that were developed for herding, including border collies, have lines that are skilled in herding. They have the stock sense and the work ethic. However, there are other lines in the breed that do not have the skills or the work ethic, and they would rather be pampered like show dogs than work. God has endowed us all with abilities to serve Him in some capacity, but we must be willing to hone and use those gifts for His purpose. As Paul writes in 2 Timothy 2:20-21: "In a large house there are articles not only of gold and silver, but also of wood and clay; some are for noble purposes and some for ignoble. If a man cleanses himself from the latter, he will be an instrument for noble purposes, made holy, useful to the Master and prepared to do any good work" (NIV).

Questions to Ponder

1. Have you found or identified your God-given purpose? If so, are you fulfilling that purpose for God?

   My purpose is to be an encourager and a "Hope Dealer" to hurting people.

2. Do you struggle with obedience to the Master? Is it open defiance or apathy?

   I struggle in caring for myself with my eating, exercising & disciplines

3. When God closes a door (so to speak), do you look for an open window or do you mope and complain?

   I think I look for the window

4. Do you ever feel jealous of another's success in working for the Master, or do you seek to find that same success through obedience to the Master?

   I just want to strengthen my own "serve".

CHAPTER 4 JUNEBUG

Junebug is my first border collie. She was already fully trained and keen to work, as you learned in the previous chapter. Her first owner sent her to be trained by my trainer, and then she sat in a crate or a small yard with that owner. The trainer found out about it and got her back; however, with all the dogs the trainer had, there were plenty of dogs ahead of Junebug with more experience and skill, so her working opportunities were still limited. That is until I got her. At the time I got Junebug, I had more free time in my schedule and we were on the sheep field practicing and herding a minimum of three times a week; more often, it was five days.

When I got Junebug, she knew quite a bit more than I did, but she was so biddable and eager to work that she had patience with me. Junebug wanted to work, so she listened to me, but she also let me know when I was misreading the sheep or the draw. She would stop and look at me as if to say, "Are you sure?" If I repeated the command, she was obedient, and then I'd see what she saw as they responded the way she anticipated. Junebug has always had stock sense: she could anticipate and make corrections on the fly. When I realized that fact, I was more willing to trust her when she questioned my commands. She would correct lines for me and let me know when sheep were through an obstacle.

In the beginning my timing was off, as I was not that great at watching my sheep. As my timing improved and the more often I was correct, the more she trusted me. When I caused her to *lose her sheep* with bad timing and wrong commands, she would get tense, but she kept working for me, with me. Losing her sheep meant I moved her away from covering *the draw* (the direction the sheep want to go) and the sheep would take off running. When my timing and commands were right, it helped her to relax knowing that together we were less likely to lose the sheep. We soon became a team.

There were times along the way that she took over for me, because I didn't know what I was doing and she got anxious. I had to learn to be careful that I did not let her take over because she was ready and willing to do so. However, I am the master, and, therefore, obedience is expected. As a handler and a shepherd I was very green and, in the beginning, it was real easy to get my flank commands mixed up (*clockwise Come by – and counter clock wise —Away*). So, when I gave her a flank command opposite what it should have been, she would give me the look. As I developed my skills in sheepherding and handling, Junebug and I became a team. We had confidence in each other's abilities, and we worked together, each doing our part.

From the beginning, she was extremely attentive to where I was and what I was wanting. Once it was clear in her head what I was wanting or doing, she would help me to get that done. For example, gate-sorting is not an easy task, but with an obedient and focused dog, it can be done without a lot of stress on either the handler/shepherd or the sheep. The sorting process makes it possible for the shepherd to get the specific sheep needed and separate them from the flock. Working as a team, the dog will bring the sheep to the gate or to the shepherd and hold the sheep while the shepherd sorts them.

When I was learning to gate-sort, I was given the task of getting the white sheep separated from the black sheep. Junebug figured out I was wanting white sheep, and she was more diligent about keeping the black ones back from the gate. Then the task changed to sorting the black sheep out. Again, Junebug realized what I was doing, and she held back the white ones. Sorting and shedding require more concentration on the part of the dog to follow the commands given. Yet, the dog is ready in a split second to move as directed to be successful in culling the ones chosen by the shepherd/handler or directed by the judge in a sheepdog trial. As I became more confident and more competent as a handler, Junebug became more trusting of my commands, and she did not question my judgement as she had in the beginning. In her initial training, she locked on to the fact that the master/handler wanted to send sheep between panels on a course. So anytime there are panels between the sheep and the handler, Junebug makes every effort to get them through right down the middle between the panels. Not every dog recognizes that part of the course, and the handler must work harder to direct the dog where to be to get the sheep through panels.

The other fascinating thing about Junebug is her *eye*. She, essentially, stares at the sheep with a look to say, "Oh no you don't," or "You better move." She has always worked quietly and is kind to her sheep, but that focused stare lets them know she means business, and they don't argue with her. *The eye* is a characteristic found in many border collies and is quite effective in convincing sheep on who is in control.

Papers and Back breeding

Junebug's daddy has Irish blood, and her back breeding has Irish imports on both the mother and father's side. I sat with an Irish shepherd who was judging an SDT (sheepdog trial). He recognized every dog in her back breeding, and he said she was from well-bred herding lines. Her genealogy is strictly herding, not confirmation. There is a difference, which I will explain.

Confirmation versus Herding

Dogs with American Kennel Club (AKC) confirmation are bred selecting for physical characteristics, such as larger heads, shorter legs, and more fluff in the coat. Many of those dogs are trained for agility or fly ball, along with confirmation shows. The American Border Collie Association (ABCA) herding lines select for speed, flexible joints, the desire to head (go to the head of the sheep to turn them), eye, and stamina.

In fact, there was a book written called *The Dog Wars* by Donald McCaig about the proponents of each side striving to control the breeding. It became so heated that to preserve the herding lines and characteristics for which they were created, any ABCA dog that is entered in AKC confirmation will have their registration papers revoked. It is so noted on the bottom of the ABCA registration certificate.

Border collies are generally people-pleasers and will perform in whatever role they are given. But when you see a border collie that has been doing another sport exposed to herding for the first time, it is like a light goes on. *So, this is living!*

The sad fact is although we have been created for a purpose, if we are not careful, we too can find ourselves at the mercy of external forces pressing us into service we are ill-suited for. Have you ever felt yourself longing to serve in other ways or ministries than the ones you are currently serving? If so, you may not be using your gifts to the full extent. Pray about it and God will lead you in the path He has set for you.

LESSON 2

You cannot <u>manipulate</u> change in others; it will diminish their gifts. Change must come from the <u>desire</u> within.

God created us in His image, endowed us with gifts, and gave us purpose. He does not force change; He loves us and calls us to service.

Purpose

My border collie Junebug was bred for one specific purpose: to herd sheep. It is her responsibility to go find and retrieve the sheep, to bring them straight to me, or hold them in a straight line that I have designated to take the sheep where I need them.

When I am sorting sheep, she must recognize which ones I am wanting and hold those for me. It is imperative that I communicate clearly so she knows where we are going and what we are doing. She must take my commands and stop on a dime. Together, we became competitive with professional handlers. As long as she is fulfilling her purpose, she is happy, healthy, and bright-eyed. But if you remove her from the sheep field too long, she gets restless.

Border collies have been found to understand phrases and whole sentences. It is remarkable. They respond to the tone of voice and whistle, and listen intently for any variations to adjust their course. Consequently, boredom can lead to destructive and unwanted behaviors: digging and shredding paper, curiosity that gets them into trouble, etc. But if they have the opportunity to work sheep several times a week, they are content; they'll rest comfortably in their crate, even with the door open. They often prefer being in their "dens" to reduce overstimulation. They are happy; better yet, they do not want to engage in unwanted behaviors.

We too have a purpose. When we are following God's will for our lives, we are challenged and we grow. We readily develop more "Fruit of the Spirit" (see Galatians 5:22-23) rather than indulging in inappropriate or sluggard behaviors. We feel at peace and sleep is sweet. We work hard, and we know we are becoming the people God destined us to be. With God, there are no mistakes or miscues if we are paying attention to the path He has set for us. That is if we take care of the responsibilities and the tasks we are equipped for. There is nothing sweeter than fulfilling God's purpose in your life – it flows. There will be peaks and valleys, but He is always calling you to the work and to Him.

LESSON 3

Nothing is sweeter than fulfilling God's <u>purpose</u> in your life. He is always <u>calling</u> you to the work and to Him.

Paul reminds us of this in Romans 8:28-30 (NIV):

> And we know that in all things God works for the good of those who love him, who have been called according to his purpose. For those God foreknew he also predestined to be conformed to the likeness of his Son, that he might be the firstborn among many brothers. And those he predestined, he also called; those he called, he also justified; those he justified, he also glorified.

Vetted

Not only was Junebug bred for sheepherding with strong back breeding from Ireland, but she was thoroughly vetted during my thirty-day trial. Vetting has come to mean a thorough examination and scrutiny by an expert to identify whether the animal or individual is acceptable or approved to work. Bloodwork was done, a heartworm test, parasite screening, examined for Collie Eye and Hip Dysplasia, all to determine she was sound. A hearing test is usually performed as well. Once the veterinarian was certain she was healthy, with good muscle tone and disease-free, I made the final decision to keep her and write the check.

I am often thankful that God does not subject us to such scrutiny before allowing us to be saved; yet, He does indeed provide periods of testing to refine us to be appropriate for the task at hand.

David tells us: "The LORD is in his holy temple; the LORD is on his heavenly throne. He observes the sons of men; his eyes examine them. The LORD examines the righteous, but the wicked and those who love violence his soul hates" (Ps. 11:4-5 NIV). Notice it says He examines the righteous – He loves us so much He will discipline and refine us. Solomon reminds us, "For a man's ways are in full view of the LORD, and he examines all his paths" (Prov. 5:21 NIV). David goes so far as to ask for the scrutiny in Psalm 26:2 (NIV): "Test me, O LORD, and try me, examine my heart and my mind."

Training

Even though the border collie has been bred for all the right characteristics and instinct necessary for herding livestock, they must still be trained. Training entails development of their natural talent and skills, but channeled to be kind to the sheep. Proper training requires consistency and a sense of fairness from the trainer.

The dog must learn to follow directions, literally to know his right from his left, and to change directions on command. They must be taught how to hold pressure; in other words, to cover the draw (*the way the sheep want to go*). Dogs must learn that the shepherd and master is always in control. They need to learn how to move the sheep in a straight line and hold the line the master has set. It is imperative they learn to pace themselves to move the sheep without chasing and to keep them moving. Otherwise, the sheep will take off running in fear.

Border collies must learn to respond to sheep challenges or attempts to veer off course, either subtly with their eye, with their body and presence, or with direct head-to-head confrontation if required. A "nice dog" will be alert to what went wrong, causing the sheep to get away from it and will make an adjustment on his own to avoid the same scenario. Junebug is a "nice dog"!

Ten Commands

1. Look/ Just Look

This tells the dog to look up and across the field to spot the position of the sheep, but to wait for further instructions before moving. With this command, the dog, once it has spotted the sheep, is to be at the ready when sent. We too must be watching for and recognizing "lost sheep" among us.

2. Come bye Here/ Come – The *sheep are the clock.* Go left or clockwise around ...*we call that flanking.*

3. Away to Me /Away – Go right or counterclockwise.

4. Lie Down / Stand – Stop immediately and wait there for the next command. **Stand** allows the dog to remain on its feet to exhibit more power to the sheep. One of the hardest and most important lessons for the dog to learn is to stop on command. Regardless of where the sheep are, whether they take off or stand still, ***the dog must stop.*** Many dogs find that hard to do, especially in the beginning. They are afraid that if the sheep get away from them, they may not be able to catch them. Sometimes it is a fear they will be trampled if asked to lie down just feet away from on-looking sheep. Other times they are obedient and responsive while up close to the master, but at a distance they choose to take matters into their own hands. In the beginning, for the protection of the sheep, it is necessary to use a long line (*rope attached to the dog*) in training sessions. When the dog is asked to lie down, the shepherd can step on the rope or jerk it as necessary to insist on obedience to the command. If the dog does not stop, the shepherd will run to the sheep and take possession to keep the dog off. Then the dog is removed from the field and told, "You lost your sheep because you wouldn't listen." They lose the opportunity to work and serve the master; worse, the master is displeased. The ultimate correction for a sheepdog, especially a border collie, is to take away his sheep. Depending on how defiant the dog is or how many times the dog refused to stop, he can find himself on lockdown. This means the dog is crated except for bathroom breaks, with no play time with other dogs or the master. And instead of freedom, he finds himself on the end of a leash.

When you hear the Spirit of God directing you in your heart, do you stop and listen or just keep moving? I must admit one of the most difficult things for me to do is to be still. I can be dog tired, excuse the pun, but I push myself on to finish or do more. When I am really honest with myself, I can look back and see that had I stopped, I'd have been better off. Now, I have more work because I was not as conscientious and attentive to detail. Worse, I find myself far afield of where the Master placed me. I can get back there but it takes time, and sometimes I miss the opportunity or the blessing that would have come had I stopped. That is a perfect example of being in the wrong place at the wrong time. Sometimes it does not seem like that big of a deal; it is only a few steps more. Yet, the point is I am not in control;

God, the Master of the Universe, is. I must not try to second guess His direction and purpose.

LESSON 4

Learn <u>patience</u> and <u>self-control</u> so you can persevere.

I know we joke about not praying for patience, because it means we will be given ample opportunities to practice patience. But how else can we grow? I believe of the virtues of the Fruit of the Spirit, "patience" is the most difficult to grasp; and the attribute most visible to others observing our behavior. It makes all the difference in a relationship.

Patience and self-control are so important to our Christian character that God inspired several writers in both the New and Old Testament to drive the point home. I love how James, the brother of Jesus, said it in James 5:7-8 (NIV): "Be **patient**, then, brothers, until the LORD's coming. See how the farmer waits for the land to yield its valuable crops and how **patient** he is for autumn and spring rains. You too, be **patient** and stand firm, because the LORD's coming is near." Job referred to it as well: "Teach me, and I will be quiet; show me where I have been wrong" (Job 6:24 NIV). Paul offers a comparative example as he writes to the church in Thessalonica: "So then, let us not be like others, who are asleep, but let us be alert and self-controlled" (1 Thess. 5:6 NIV).

There are also commands that dictate the pace and direction down to a few steps. Such commands change the trajectory of a large flank to move the sheep exactly where the shepherd wants them.

5. Walk-Up

Get up immediately and move forward at a trot or canter to push the sheep away from a draw.

6. Steady

Get up slowly and walk toward the sheep. Pace yourself so that you are out of the bubble (proximity in relation to the sheep that does not make them uncomfortable or skittish), but calmly moving them forward or holding a line.

7. There

Turn in toward the sheep now!

8. Here/ Here Here

Calling the dog to the master like the command **come** in obedience training.

Sometimes the dog anticipates what the handler will do and starts making his own decisions when to stop, to turn the sheep, where to go next.

On occasion, the way the handler or master is sending just does not make sense – remember we may never understand why or what is happening. At times, we are headed in the right direction, but we have missed a fork in the road or a turn off or, more importantly, we are far afield of where the Master wants us to be. We must be extremely careful; the Shepherd alone knows the plan. We need to be as attentive to detail as the Master, and we cannot do it without the guidance of the Holy Spirit. Read Jeremiah 10:23 (NIV): "I know, O LORD, that a man's life is not his own; it is not for man to direct his steps." Also, Proverbs 16:9 (NIV): "In his heart a man plans his course, but the LORD determines his steps." The writers make it clear the path is determined and directed by our Master, the Sovereign LORD Himself.

9. Look Back

This command tells the dog to look back or look around because a sheep has left the group or is lagging. **Look Back** is also used to let the dog know there is another group of sheep that the dog needs to gather.

Once, we were at an SDT where the fields being used were fairly close together, only about 200 yards apart. Consequently, whistles being blown on one field were heard by dogs working the other field. In one case, the dog had lifted the sheep and was headed toward the handler when it heard its "**look back**" whistle. At that point, the dog stopped and started looking back to see if there were more sheep to go back for. Unfortunately, the dog was so distracted by the "foreign whistle" that it took some time for the handler to redirect it back on course bringing the sheep; and during the confusion, the sheep took off and had to be gathered again. To get the dog's attention, the handler blew the "Lie down" whistle for the dog to just BE STILL and listen. I believe that happens to us as well. We know God's voice and we know He's giving us direction, but we get conflicting directions from Satan that get us all in a dither because we get distracted, turned around, and don't know what to do. At that point, the only way I can calm down and know what to do is to BE STILL and wait for God or His Spirit to redirect me.

10. That'll Do. We'll discuss at the end.

I love the way David talks to our Lord requesting guidance; this should be our constant prayer.

> Teach me, O LORD, to follow your decrees;
> then I will keep them to the end. Give me

understanding, and I will keep your law and obey it with all my heart. Direct me in the path of your commands, for there I find delight (Psalms 119:33 -35 NIV).

Focus

For the sheepdog, focus is a key to staying on task, getting the job done, ignoring distractions, and following the shepherd home. Junebug is endowed with a desire to please the shepherd, as well as the skill in reading the stock to herd them wherever the shepherd wants them. She always has her eye on the sheep when they are present, in addition to looking to me for commands and direction. She is focused to such an extent that when she is working, physical distractions such as sex drive and pain do not deter her from her work.

One summer, Jewel, Angelica (another handler), and I were working our dogs on a fallow field that had become covered in stickers during the drought. The first time we took the dogs out, we were not aware of the stickers. I ran Junebug and she worked as she always did. When I sent her to water, I noticed she was licking her feet. I checked her paws one by one and each of them were covered in stickers some three layers deep. She never flinched or stopped to pull them out. Jewel's dog ran next, and he kept stopping to pull stickers out of his paws. Angelica's dog also ran and then came in limping with the stickers. We combed that field and the stickers were everywhere. We drug blankets behind the truck with a heavy chain on it to pull them out. We walked around with towels wrapped around our boots, but we could not get them all. We tried putting booties on their paws and wrapped their feet loosely with vet wrap and put duct tape on the bottom over it. All the dogs felt hampered by the "paw protection;" they preferred to run without protection and then get them out at the end. Once it was clear they refused to let us protect their paws, we quit going to that field.

I have seen dogs that have sliced their pads, pulled a muscle, or with a thorn in their foot continue to work as they have been trained. Often the shepherd is not aware of their discomfort or injury until long after the work is done. Then, and only then, will they limp or lick their wounds, allowing the handler to provide comfort, binding their wounds, removing thorns or quills, and administering pain killer or muscle relaxants as needed.

Solomon spoke of focus in his book of wisdom, Proverbs:

> Let your eyes look straight ahead, fix your
> gaze directly before you. Make
> level paths for your feet and take only ways
> that are firm. Do not swerve to
> the right or the left; keep your foot from evil.
> (Proverbs 4:25-27 NIV).

LESSON 5

<u>Fix</u> your eyes on the Master. <u>Focus</u> on the lost sheep He has sent you to bring home.

I have seen an intact male and female trying desperately to get the opportunity to copulate when the female is in standing heat; however, once they were sent to work the sheep, the focus totally changed, and they were just as effective and disciplined working the sheep as they are without raging pheromones.

I heard the story of a dog that was struck by a copperhead while working sheep around some cedar brush, unbeknownst to the handler until the dog's head began to swell. There was no yelp, whimper, or refusal to work. That is true focus and trust that the shepherd will provide the needed care once the work is done. *It should be noted that working dogs are given rattlesnake vaccines annually, which greatly reduces the effect of venom from various snakes. With such vaccines, the end result is a happy one.*

Unlike the human shepherd, God knows when we will face, and are facing, danger, or when we are in pain and in great need of His care. NOTHING IS A SURPRISE to GOD! I am reminded of the verses of Solomon in Proverbs. "Trust in the LORD with all your heart and lean not on your own understanding; in all your ways acknowledge him, and he will make your paths straight" (Prov. 3:5-6 NIV). What a blessing to have in our LORD, God such an omniscient and omnipotent shepherd!

Eye on the Prize

I believe that this is the type of focus we should have to the task and calling the Father has endowed us with and, more importantly, a clear focus on God, our Creator and Savior. Sadly, all too often I may find myself with that kind of focus on something superficial or attractive, and I am not waiting or listening for the call or urging of the Master to refocus on Him and the task at hand. Peter found himself focusing on distancing himself from danger rather than owning up to his relationship with Christ. The Bible says, "Then Peter remembered the words Jesus had spoken: 'Before the rooster crows, you will disown me three times'" (Matt. 26:75 NIV). Peter, remembering the words of Jesus and his for certain betrayal, went out from where he was and wept bitterly. Thankfully, Jesus is very aware of our human frailties and weaknesses, and He gave Peter another chance by entrusting him with the care of His people. I love the tenderness of Jesus when He reinstated Peter. John included it in his gospel:

When they had finished eating, Jesus said to Simon Peter, "Simon son of John, do you truly love me more than these?" "Yes, LORD," he said, "you know that I love you." Jesus said, **"Feed my lambs."** Again Jesus said, "Simon son of John, do you truly love me?" He answered, "Yes, LORD, you know that I love you." Jesus said, **"Take care of my sheep."** The third time he said to him, "Simon son of John, do you love me?" Peter was hurt because Jesus asked him the third time," Do you love me?" He said, "LORD, you know all things, you know that I love you." Jesus said, **"Feed my sheep**...Then he said to him, **"Follow me!"** (John 21:15-19 NIV)

Eye

Border collies have been bred over time to head the sheep, which means they will face down the sheep, head to head, as it were in a crouch position. That breeding has developed more confidence and forward momentum in the dog's ability to herd. Those bloodlines are present in dogs with "eye" or the dog's use of communicating to the sheep through the eyes: "I'm in charge," "Don't you dare," "Move," "Don't even think about it." I have seen Junebug working sheep down a fence line. She looks to the leader to tell them to stop or slow down, and she looks back to the straggler to get with the group. It's quite impressive to see especially when it is done in a crouch position; but believe me, the sheep readily understand and move accordingly. Sometimes the dogs will "eye up" and be frozen, unable to move. If the handler does not quickly and regularly require the dog to disengage the "eye," the dog will become "sticky" and ineffective in moving sheep. It is a fine line how much eye he can appropriately use to fetch or drive the sheep; there has to be a look he gives the sheep to let them know he is in charge and the sheep cannot escape.

At the same time, his eye will cause him to come in too close on a flank because he is following his head. In those instances, the shepherd will tell the dog to "get out of that" or say, "what are you doing in here?" Both phrases can be used if they coincide with the flank direction; one to remind them they are wrong on the right side and the other on the left. The Spirit does that for us if we are listening.

Mark and Luke both remind us to be listening in their gospels. Mark 13: 32-33 (NIV): "No one knows about that day or hour, not even the angels in heaven, nor the Son, but only the Father. Be on guard! Be alert! You do not know when that time will come." And "It will be good for those servants whose master finds them watching when he comes" (Luke 12:37 NIV).

Eyed-Up or Sticky

Sometimes we set our sights on the wrong thing. Junebug has a lot of eye and when she locks on the cat, a stuffed animal, or even sheep, her fixation will cause her to lose sight of the job. She knows instinctively that sheep, like us, have a *bubble* or personal space. When that boundary or space is invaded, the sheep will run or scatter.

A dog that becomes eyed-up does not respect the boundary, and, therefore, is not effective in moving the sheep in a kind and quiet manner, methodical and controlled. Instead, he dives in like a flyby; he buzzes the sheep, sending them running. Or, if the dog becomes sticky, he may stand frozen, regardless of the command given, allowing the sheep to go where they want. Worse, the dog can become fixated on something as simple as a stuffed animal. It takes a lot of energy to maintain attention and focus for extended periods of time, and yet fixation can become a type of *mental and psycho physical* paralysis.

When Junebug goes into my office at home, I have a lot of stuffed sheep; and I must remind her not to fixate on those inanimate objects. When Alyssa, my granddaughter, and I traveled to a sheepdog trial (competition), she had to hide her stuffed animal so Junebug would not stare at it. There is no purpose; in staring at a toy sheep, energy is wasted, and if not careful, such focus can be *dangerous.* It causes her to lose sight of the big picture and the purpose for which she was designed. The psalmist refers to this in Psalm 141:4 (NIV): "Let not my heart be drawn toward what is evil, to take part in wicked deeds with men who are evil doers; let me not eat of their delicacies."

Focus on Purpose

I wish I could say that I never find myself stuck on the wrong thing. The truth of the matter is it is all too easy to perseverate on something trivial rather than the real task or mission I was given. Do you ever find yourself with a big job that will take a full commitment to complete; however, you keep finding things that have nothing to do with the task catching your eye?

Satan and this world provide all kinds of alluring distractions, some to entangle us in sin and others to simply deter us from God's purpose. All too often we don't consider the source of the distraction or we feel we are in control, and yet if our eyes are not focused on the Master and the task at hand no matter what we tell ourselves, we are missing the mark. Satan was bold enough to confront our Master and Shepherd face to face, although he waited until he thought he was weak after a 40 day and night fast in the desert. If he is willing to confront the Master head on, what makes us think we will be any different? Satan missed that even though Jesus' body was in a weakened state after the intense desert heat and His fasting; Jesus' mind, His Spirit and His focus were fixed on God and His sovereign purpose.

I don't believe Satan acknowledges the power of a spiritual fast – it's not just depriving the body of food; it is grasping hold of the Holy Spirit to discern God's will and purpose for that time in our lives. I know in my case that if I'm fasting for the purpose of losing weight, all I can think about is how hungry I am and how good the food around me looks. However, if I am fasting to pull closer to God and strengthen the bond between my soul and His Spirit, food is the last thing on my mind. It is all about the focus.

Our Master and Shepherd was confronted with human suffering both physical and spiritual all around Him, in the crowds, in His disciples and even His physical family. He could have healed all their physical suffering. He is God, but that was not His focus or the purpose God the Father sent Him here to fulfill. To maintain that focus, and be obedient to His purpose, Christ Jesus spent precious time in prayer alone with God. Take a look at His example in Mark 1:35-38:

Very early in the morning, while it was still dark, Jesus got up, left the house and went off to a solitary place, where he prayed. Simon and his companions went to look for him, they exclaimed: "Everyone is looking for you!" Jesus replied, "Let us go somewhere else – to the nearby villages – so I can preach there also. That is why I have come" (NIV).

Think about it: To maintain our relationship and be obedient to the Master our first priority is Bible reading, praying, meditating, studying, and memorizing Scripture. Is it any wonder we are worn down, with everything bombarding us? Don't misunderstand me; I believe there should be a sense of urgency in spending time in the Word, but God doesn't force us to make time for Him. We must choose to do that on our own. We must go away to a solitary place and spend time with the Shepherd. There is no better way to prevent stress and burnout than with Him.

I am ashamed to say that when I sit down to read my Bible, if I'm not careful, I find myself getting up to take care of this and that. This ends in no time to read the Bible until late in the day, unless I read it online on break at work. How much meditation and benefit can I get in snippets of time – honestly none, because my focus is wrong or at the very least split. But if I start my day in the Word, I'm ready to face the challenges ahead because I've spent time with the Master. And when it's time to rest, I'll be able to do so.

Questions to Ponder

1. Think about your heritage in the faith. Can you see God's plan and purpose for you specifically to get you where you are today?

   _____

   _____

2. How would you classify your level of obedience to God? Do you live to serve?

   _____

   _____

3. Do you feel you have been vetted for service in His kingdom?

   _____

   _____

4. What holds your focus? Do you find yourself getting stuck on worthless endeavors?

   _____

   _____

CHAPTER 5
GO-TO DOG

Work Ethic

A good sheepdog is always ready to work. The work, no matter the season, how big or small the job is does not matter. They know the importance of getting every last sheep, no matter the risk. Sometimes the dogs cannot see the sheep when the master sends them. But the master has never lied to them, if the dogs are sent; it means there are sheep out there. They will run out at top speed, looking, searching for the sheep, but always attentive to the master's direction because the master always knows where the sheep are. There is trust and confidence in the master so all they must do is their part. They do not have to try to figure out where to take the sheep or what the plan is; they simply follow the commands and instructions given. They hold the line until the command comes to change it. They want very much to please the master and are looking for his praise and encouragement.

God sends us out to gather in the fields, bring home the strays and search for the lost. God knows exactly where they are, and He directs our steps to cross the path with those who are lost and dying. We, like the sheepdogs, are seeking

God's approval and blessing, and we work hard to stay in His good grace.

Go-to Dog

Although I have two border collies for sheepherding, when I need help with the sheep, Junebug is my "go-to dog." I know she is always ready to work and will listen. There is no doubt in my mind that when I send her, she will go where I send her and will do what I ask of her. I will not have to beg her or argue with her; she knows the job and is faithful to complete the work.

I pray that I can be the Master's go-to just as the prophets in the Old Testament state. Isaiah 6:8 says, "Then I heard the voice of the Lord saying, 'Whom shall I send? And who will go for us?' And I said, 'Here am I. Send me!'" (NIV). Also, 1 Samuel 3:4 says, "Then the Lord called Samuel. Samuel answered, 'Here I am'" (NIV).

Looking for Opportunities

The reason Junebug was chosen for the task is that she is always alert and looking for opportunities to serve. When we arrive at the sheep field, she jumps out and starts scanning the field for sheep. Once she has found them, she will lie down or stand, still focused on the sheep. Junebug is very sociable and loves to play with other dogs. Yet, she knows there is a time and a place for everything. So as long as there are sheep in the field, she stands at the ready. After the sheep have been moved to the barnyard or feed pen and locked up, she will look to me as if to say, "Is that all?" Paul encourages us to be that ready and willing, "Therefore, my dear brothers, stand firm. Let nothing move you. Always give yourselves fully to the work of the LORD, because you know that your labor in the LORD is not in vain" (1 Cor. 15:58 NIV).

LESSON 6

Be <u>ready</u> when the Master calls and <u>give it all</u> you've got.

Paul again tells us in Ephesians 5:15-17 (NIV),

> Be very careful, then, how you live – not as unwise but as wise, making the most of every opportunity, because the days are evil. Therefore do not be foolish, but understand what the LORD's will is.

Hold the Line

Oh how I want my focus to be right, to be keen, and to be immovable. When driving sheep (*pushing, moving them away from the shepherd*) with a dog, I have been told countless times that I must watch my sheep. Good handling means that I am aware of the dog and its position and proximity to the sheep. However, if I do not keep a watchful eye on the sheep, they will drift or stray to the left or to the right. The slightest movement of the lead sheep's head can direct the sheep away from the desired course. It takes a keen eye and real focus not only to command the dog or redirect when it appears to be changing the course back toward me, rather than a drive-away, but also pay attention to the sheep. If I lose sight of the end point and the sheep, my aim will be off and the drive will be sloppy and harried, certainly not a straight path. When I watch my sheep and endpoint to which I am driving, the lines are straight and the path is direct – a thing of beauty to behold.

I am so thankful that God always has His eye on me and all of His sheep as well as the end goal. It is true, indeed, that He makes my paths straight. I love that God knows we cannot measure up on our own, and He makes Himself present to lead and guide us. As stated in Proverbs 3:5-6 (NIV), "Trust in the LORD with all your heart and lean not on your own understanding; in all your ways acknowledge him, and he will make your paths straight."

Call to Be Still

There are times the master requires the dog to lie down, even up close to settle the sheep or to hold the sheep in a specific spot. Sheep are bigger than the dogs to start with, and lying down is *a submissive posture.* Therefore, it takes a lot of confidence and courage to listen to the master and look up into those sheep faces. The dog is aware that at any time, a sheep could decide to charge, to stomp, or head-butt the dog.

Yet, obedience to the master is more important to the sheepdog than the risk. The dog has come to know the master is always watching, ready to step in and help. It is a relationship of trust. The instinct of the dog is to stay on its feet, to keep sheep moving, to push them or bring them, certainly not to lie down, and hold the position no matter what.

LESSON 7

The following quote is apropos: "The lifetime lesson learned from working with Lass was simply this: **Faith is my personal, positive response to the Word of God, to the point where I act in quiet trust**" (Keller, 1983, 2002). Taken from <u>Lessons From A Sheep Dog <i>A True Story of Transforming Love</i></u> by Phillip Keller Copyright © 1983, 2002 by W. Phillip Keller. Used by permission of Thomas Nelson, www.thomasnelson.com. pg.26.

Till the Job is Done

There is a time and a place for everything, including rest and refreshment. For working dogs in sheepherding, the best ones have a lot of heart and a strong work ethic. That is Junebug; she will continue to work until she is called off the sheep. As her master, I have to be watchful that Junebug doesn't overheat, especially working Texas summers in 100° degree temperatures during the heat of the day. A border collie will often hide how hot it is until it is called off the sheep; at that point, it relaxes its tongue and the master has an opportunity to see how big the dog's tongue is as it droops from its mouth in panting.

Often, Junebug will not show how hot she is until the sheep are penned or the job is done, but with dehydration sometimes, her panting will lather up and give her away. I have seen other dogs that worked until they became wobbly and dropped from exhaustion. It is especially important to let the dog know you are pleased with her efforts or her work. A dog will work a long time on a little bit of encouragement and grace from the master; so will we. Paul tells us to have a lot of heart in Colossians 3:23 (NIV), "Whatever you do, work at it with all your heart, as working for the LORD, not for men." Junebug has a lot of heart as well.

Go to Water

Once I see that big tongue on Junebug, I send her to water. But sometimes she is very aware the work is not done, and I am still working. That being the case, she will start toward the water tank or tub and then come back to me to keep working. On those days, I must physically walk her over to the water and command her to get in and stay there.

Sometimes, dogs may need to soak in the water and lap it up for as long as twenty minutes before the tongue shrinks back to normal and they are physically ready to work again.

A real attentive master will send the dog to water in the middle of a task for a quick refresher, and then back into the fray while the shepherd holds the sheep. Once the dog realizes that a short rest is possible and the dog will again be called on to serve, the dog will more readily accept the break and the rest.

God does not expect us to work until we can work no more or until we are exhausted. He provides opportunities along the way to enjoy pools of refreshing water and rest. Sometimes, we press ourselves longer and harder than we should, and may become injured in the process because our guard was down. We did not take care of ourselves, or we made stupid mistakes because we didn't think we were so tired. In those instances, God will have to physically move us to water and make us stay there to heal or recover if necessary. It is so much better to follow the Shepherd's example and withdraw to a solitary place and rest with the Father.

Jesus taught the disciples to take time to rest and refresh, as told in both Mark and Luke's gospels. Mark 6:31-32 (NIV):

Then, because so many people were coming and going that they did not even have a chance to eat, he said to them, "Come with me by yourselves to a quiet place and get some rest." So they went away by themselves in a boat to a solitary place.

And Luke 9:10 (NIV): "When the apostles returned, they reported to Jesus what they had done. Then he took them with him, and they withdrew by themselves to a town called Bethsaida."

LESSON 8

That'll do

1. Stop what you are doing

The task is complete and there is no need to work the sheep any further.

2. Return to the Master

"That'll do" is actually the recall for working sheepdogs. The dog is expected to go to the master immediately. My dogs know that I will be sending them to water; but first, I have praise for a job well done.

3. Rest is waiting

Now is the time to cool off and take a deep breath. Once Junebug is cooled off, she shakes the water off at a distance and then returns to my side.

The Shepherd calls us to Him as He tells us:

Come to me, all you who are weary and burdened, and I will give you rest.

Take my yoke upon you and learn from me, for I am gentle and humble in heart, and you will find rest for your souls. For my yoke is easy and my burden is light (Matt. 11:28-30 NIV).

At the Master's side

Whenever I am at home, Junebug will come into the room where I am and lie down beside me. She just wants to be close; of course, she would love petting, but she is content just being with me. She is the only one that is always there waiting, with me. Tux is doing whatever he can find to do, and if Rascal is not wrestling with Tux, she is hanging out in her crate. Both Tux and Rascal will come in from time to time and beg for petting. But unless they are given a command to lie down and stay, they will soon leave. Not Junebug, she will be there beside me for hours, whether I am in the house or outside in the garden. In fact, Kip can be petting her when I come home, and she immediately leaves him to come to my side.

Walk with the Master

Like Junebug, I love the thought of being close to the Master. I often imagine He walks with me in the cool of the evening; I just have to look up. In His presence, I feel comfort, safety, and LOVE. Sleep is sweet when He is close at hand, especially if I've worked hard in service that day. I could not ask for anything better. THANK YOU, FATHER!

Questions to Ponder

1. Have you made yourself ready and available to God to be the one He sends?

   _____

   _____

2. Do you find it difficult to walk a straight path, without giving into the distracting world around you?

   _____

   _____

3. How hard is it for you to be still? Can you keep your mind clear and focused when you are still, or do you find it racing?

   _____

   _____

4. Can you identify with the Phillip Keller quote? "Faith is my personal, positive response to the Word of God, to the point where I act in quiet trust"?

   _____

   _____

CHAPTER 6

RASCAL

In the spring of 2014, I got another border collie named Rascal. She would be three years in June of that year and finally mature enough to train and handle the pressure of training on sheep. Her owner gave up on her because she was soft. Soft dogs can be frustrating because they simply do not respond well to harsh voices or discipline.

I wanted another dog, so I was willing to send her for training and see if she would work out. I could at least give her thirty days, the regular length of a trial period before purchase.

Papers & Back breeding

In Rascal's case, much of her back breeding is English and Scottish for three generations. She exhibits much more of the characteristics of her English/ Scottish ancestors in the way she works. Quite different from Junebug, she has more push and power but less "eye." She is what they call an upright dog; she does not crouch like Junebug, but stands erect.

Equipped for the Purpose

Rascal was bred from four generations of champions, going back to her Scottish and English roots. Dusty, her mom, was a champion here in Texas and competed all over the United States. Her DNA includes instinct:

1) To walk into faces of the sheep and turn them, *called heading.*
2) To spot sheep at a distance.

60

3) To respond to the slightest movement or twitch, *indicating a sheep is ready to break away.*

4) To bring the sheep straight to the master.

We too have been endowed with skills and gifts to do the Master's bidding, bringing in the lost sheep. As we read in Hebrews 13:20-21 (NIV): "May the God of peace, who through the blood of the eternal covenant brought back from the dead our Lord Jesus, that great Shepherd of the sheep, <u>equip you with everything good for doing his will</u>, and may <u>he work in us what is pleasing to him,</u> through Jesus Christ, to whom be glory forever and ever. Amen."

Peter also tells us, "His divine power has given us everything we need for life and godliness through our knowledge of him who called us by his own glory and goodness" (2 Pet. 1:3 NIV).

LESSON 9

You are <u>equipped</u> for the work the Master calls you to.

Run Amuck

Unfortunately, when Rascal was a puppy, her original owner was gravely ill, so she lived in a kennel till she was six months old. At that point, she got a new owner and went from being confined in a kennel alongside other dog runs to absolute freedom on a five-acre spread. From day one, she learned how to get into the pasture and feed pen with the sheep, and essentially ran amuck. At some point, the owner started penning her up with the rest of her pack. But Rascal was like Houdini; she could figure a way out of any pen or kennel. She used her unique intelligence to develop escape routes. It is like she decided she would never again respect boundaries that were set for her. What a poor and foolish choice she made.

Along the way, she learned two things: how to work for herself and to run from sheep faces. She believed the only way to move sheep was to charge them, to chase them and to back them into a corner. The adrenaline rush must have been intense because she did it repeatedly. If the sheep did not face her, she was bold; but the minute they turned to look at her, she ran like a scared rabbit. Flop Ear, *a mean ewe,* must have rolled her a time or two before it was all said and done. So, she learned to high tail it out of there if the sheep charged her. *In fact, a dog working for itself or racing around pops the tail up, rather than tuck it under.*

By the time I got her, she was fearful, had no confidence and no desire to work sheep. She would not even look at them. Sheepdogs have been ruined this way because they have learned to do their own thing, and it was reinforced when the sheep responded.

LESSON 10

Respect the <u>boundaries</u> God has set for you. Be <u>wise</u> with the freedom He allows.

We too can run amuck, running ahead of the Master, never looking to Him for guidance or training. We are equipped for the purpose, but untrained and unwise. We cannot force people to go where we tell them, to manipulate them to do what we want; we have to learn to respect boundaries. Every creature, including us, has been endowed with innate ability, with mental capacity for learning, and equipped to serve the purpose for which we were created.

"Train a child in the way he should go, and when he is old he will not turn from it" (Prov. 22:6 NIV). "In the way he should go" is literally, "according to his [the child's] way." I would think the same is true for sheepdogs or any animal one is trying to train. Each has a different personality based on breed and disposition.

However, training is an essential part of the process to channel our efforts in the appropriate manner to be successful. That is why God provided training for us to develop our schema: through the pack, our parents or anyone else He puts in our lives to harness the energy and teach self-control. In a world with no boundaries, self-imposed or otherwise, we can find ourselves at the mercy of evil charging us, scaring us, and rendering us impotent.

At that point, we may no longer be willing to serve, no matter how equipped we are. Service requires both the skill, the knowledge, AND a willing spirit. This scenario causes me to reflect on this truth.

God indeed created us for a purpose, but He still allows for free will.

As we read in Exodus 36:2 (NIV), "Then Moses summoned Bezalel, and Oholiab and every skilled person to whom the LORD had given ability and **who was willing** to come and do the work." It is repeated in 1 Chronicles 28:21 (NIV),

"The divisions of the priests and Levites are ready for all the work on the temple of God, and **every willing man skilled in any craft** will help you in all the work. The officials and all the people will obey your every command" (*emphasis mine*).

God is so awesome and aware of our human tendencies that He equips those with gifts and skills to do His bidding; fully aware that some are unwilling to use their gifts for His purpose. God has equipped Rascal through genetics and breeding to herd sheep, but she is not always willing. I am afraid I also see that in my own life.

Refusal to Look

As we talked about with Junebug, looking for the sheep and at the sheep is paramount to the task of sheepherding. Whatever happened when Rascal worked sheep on her own as a pup really traumatized her. Poor baby did not have any formal training before I got her because she was a late bloomer. However, she had had some negative training experiences with too much pressure for her level of immaturity.

So, anytime I took her for training or to work sheep, she would look away, but never look at the sheep. It was almost as if she had decided that if she turned a blind eye, she would be relieved of her duty to work.

In Genesis 4:6-7, it describes this behavior: "Then the Lord said to Cain, 'Why are you angry? Why is your face downcast? If you do what is right, will you not be accepted? But if you do not do what is right, sin is crouching at your door; it desires to have you, but you must master it'" (NIV).

LESSON 11

The need for service does not <u>disappear</u> when you <u>fail</u> to notice.

My Shepherd died to save me. He knows the future, everything I will face. He has indeed equipped me to do His will and His work. So, why do I acquiesce or refuse when it seems to me to be a daunting task?

Distractions

Distractions are everywhere all the time and will absorb all our energy if we allow it. I don't know that Rascal made a conscious decision to busy herself with disgusting habits, like sniffing and eating sheep poop. It is the way soft dogs and immature dogs respond to pressure. But Rascal was almost three, now mature enough to take the pressure if we took it slow and methodical.

I believe we do the same thing, when we busy ourselves with anything but the task God gave us. I think we would be surprised if we considered the lengths we go to in order to avoid seeking God and following His path. We get caught up in watching others or peer pressure. That may or may not be good for us; however, it most certainly is a distraction and a time-waster. You can be certain that Satan will do his best to provide plenty of distractions to draw us off course and separate us from the love of the Master. Have you ever thought about that? Be careful of distractions.

God knows our level of maturity, and He is slow and methodical, if that is what it takes. I believe that is why we find ourselves learning the same lesson over and over. It can be frightening to step out of our comfort zones, and yet if we do not, we are doomed to live life with no purpose and no fulfillment.

LESSON 12

If you do not step out of your <u>comfort</u> zone, you are doomed to live a life with no <u>purpose</u> and no <u>fulfillment</u>.

Refocus

Working/training Rascal was exasperating and annoying, to say the least, especially when it was evident she was a very smart dog and able to do whatever I asked of her. Somehow, I needed to engage her brain to look at the sheep. She needed to be willing to look at them not only at a distance, but directly in their eyes close-up rather than turn away. Rascal had to focus on sheep and not to pout every time I made her lie down. It was difficult because she was so insecure, she did not want to lie down. She would ignore my commands. Then I'd have to correct her and she would pout, *turning her head away and not looking at me or the sheep.*

Clearly, she was so traumatized by mean old Flop Ear, a ewe that charged every dog sent to work the sheep, that she would refuse to face the sheep on her own. Every training session began with the phrase "Look at your sheep," followed by a command to walk, flank, etc. After months of work, she started to look on her own. As intelligent as she is, it must have been the most boring and least engaging exercise we did. But if a sheepdog does not focus on the sheep, it is worthless to the shepherd.

The good news is that Rascal started to be more attentive and now she looks at the sheep on her own, at least while she is waiting her turn to work. Baby steps.

Then I think about myself in my relationship with the Master. How many times does He have to remind me to re-focus? To look at the people that God has cross my path and find ways to serve **them**? I too have had negative experiences in the past with Christians. **There is truly nothing worse than a MEAN Christian.** *I borrowed that phrase from a dear sister in Christ because it fits and is so true.* Consequently, I find myself more task-oriented than people-oriented because of my insecurity. In other words, my awareness of brothers and sisters in need is secondary to what I am doing. Unfortunately, I cannot serve people if I will not look them in the eye. Looking through them or past them is just as bad. You and I must see people for who they are. They may be just as insecure as I am, which may be why God put us together.

LESSON 13

If you will not <u>focus</u> on the lost, how can the Master <u>use</u> you?

I want to be useable by the Shepherd, and I am so thankful that He is patient and longsuffering with me, reminding me of the most rudimentary social skills I have to bring people to Him.

Moses offered excuses when God called on him to serve, as we read in Exodus 4:10-13.

> Moses said to the LORD, "O LORD, I have never been eloquent, neither in the past nor since you have spoken to your servant. I am slow of speech and tongue." The LORD said to him, "Who gave man his mouth? Who makes him deaf or mute? Who gives him sight or makes him blind? Is it not I, the LORD? Now go; I will help you speak and will teach you what to say." But Moses said, "O LORD, please send someone else to do it" (NIV).

If there ever was a man created for a purpose, equipped for a purpose, it was Moses. You know the story. The good news is Moses did look at his sheep in the end, and he became invaluable to God, the Master Shepherd. I can certainly identify with Moses, and I take comfort in the fact that even when God's anger burned against him because of his reluctance, God gave him what he needed, both tangible in Aaron and intangible in His own Spirit.

The wisdom offered in Proverbs is quite convicting as well. Proverbs 24:10 (NIV) says, "If you falter in times of trouble, how small is your strength!"

Remember the Shepherd is always with us, we do not lack.

Paul reminds us in Philippians 4:13, "I can do everything through him who gives me strength" (NIV).

Refusal to Work

Rascal from the beginning showed a sluggard's perspective to obedience. If I asked her to do something she did not want to do, she would refuse or simply quit working and run for the water or a gate to get away from the work. Worse, she is what is called a "soft" dog; so, the raising of your voice is enough to scare her and have her lie down, belly up in submission.

When training and working sheepdogs, the master is aware of the dog's weaknesses and skills he or she does not yet possess; consequently, the expectation is different in regard to obedience and compliance for a learned or emerging skill. Rascal, unfortunately, would rather "give up" than obey.

Training

Early training and development of good sheepdogs includes lots of repetition, lots of opportunity to be successful, ending the session when they do well, and praising correct behavior. Training starts in small, confined spaces, such as a round pen *approximately the size of a horse corral*. As they become more familiar with the commands and have some consistency in moving the right direction in response to flank names, they graduate, as it were, to a small field.

Sheepdogs are hyper vigilant for movement of the handler, the livestock, and "the stick." Initial training uses visual cues by the direction and position of a stock-sorting stick or shepherd's crook. Proper training requires consistency and a sense of fairness from the trainer. A good trainer can recognize the difference in a dog that is confused but trying versus one that is being defiant or unwilling to submit.

Once a command is learned, it must be repeated often, and each time the trainer must require that it be followed each and every time, regardless. If the trainer lets the dog slide on occasion and requires adherence other times, the dog will begin to negotiate or "test" to see if it is truly necessary. Just like with children, if you train up a dog in the way it should work, when it is old it will not depart from it. It will be obedient and use its skill and experience to please the master.

Our Shepherd knows how hard it is to learn new things, especially outside our comfort zones, so He starts small. He is always consistent and fair with us.

Manipulation

Rascal will roll over, belly up to elicit pity, to discourage me or the trainer from continuing the work. She is using her "softness" to manipulate the master to let her slide and not demand full obedience. It is clear she knows what to do but is unwilling to try. However, when there are no sheep around and no work to be done, she is there at my side, "attentive and willing to please."

OUCH! I wish I could say that I never do that. I'm afraid that when the situation I find myself in becomes overwhelming, I too will beg off because it's too hard and I can't, *really won't,* do it. The truth is, I can be as much of a hypocrite to my Master and Shepherd as Rascal is to me.

My first book *I Am A Sheep?!?!* was completed in 2015, and *Made For A Purpose* was well underway. But I was afraid to publish it, to put myself out there. So, I decided that if God wanted it published, He would make it happen. In the meantime, I was happy teaching lessons about sheep, sheepdogs, and the Shepherd in ladies' Bible class and at ladies' days for the deaf.

I convinced myself that although God put it on my heart to share, and gave me the inspiration for applicable Scriptures, that I had done enough. God let me wallow in my fear for a while and then He started putting people in my face, telling me I need to publish. So finally, in February of 2020, I found a publisher and made a commitment. Yet, I still dragged my feet. When I finally dusted off the manuscript and started reading it, some new stories were added, and some text was revised. I faced my fears and submitted it to the publisher. When God has a plan, we must be willing to trust Him and follow, no matter what. "If God is for us, who can be against us?" (Rom. 8:31 NIV).

I Don't Want To

A dog that is fearful will show that in its posture. Sheep pick up on behaviors that show a dog's weakness. They will ignore or dis the dog at every turn. Sometimes in order to make the dog face its fear and remain with the handler in a training session, the trainer will put the dog on a long line so it cannot leave the field.

Unfortunately, when I take Rascal over to my sheep, she is very much afraid because they got tired of being chased when she was a pup and started facing her down. I was hopeful that as she learned to be more confident with experience, she would be able to let that go.

It is clear Paul was inspired to tell us that we are able to do God's will regardless of where it takes us. Paul tells Timothy the following: "All Scripture is God-breathed and is useful for teaching, rebuking, correcting and training in righteousness, so that the man of God may be thoroughly equipped for every good work" (2 Tim. 3:16-17 NIV).

Please Don't Make Me

Some dogs just cannot take the pressure and will do everything to avoid the task the master is wanting. Avoidance behaviors include running away from the sheep and the handler, stopping to relieve themselves or poop, sniffing the ground and eating sheep poop, or, at the very least, they disengage by looking away from the sheep and refuse to work.

It makes me wonder how often we do that. The work is too hard, the stress is too great; I don't want to and, worse, I'd rather do something as disgusting as eating filth rather than feeding on the Word.

Are you lying on your back, begging God your Shepherd to leave you alone and let you do only what you are willing and wanting to do? If so, GET UP and LISTEN to His voice. You were created for His purpose and gifted with the talent to succeed in His work. We are exhorted to be faithful and stick with it. See the following verses in the book of Hebrews:

So do not throw away your confidence; it will be richly rewarded. You need to persevere so that when you have done the will of God, you will receive what he has promised. For in just a very little while, "He who is coming will come and will not delay. But my righteous one will live by faith. And if he shrinks back, I will not be pleased with him." But we are not of those who shrink back and are destroyed, but of those who believe and are saved. (Hebrews 10:35-39 NIV)

It's Too Hard

The task of herding sheep for the dog can be quite difficult. Sheep may challenge a dog, stamping its feet, and even charging head down to butt or roll the dog.

The dog must "head." Not only do they need to get out in front and face the sheep, they need to exude the attitude and confidence so the sheep has no choice but to turn and go the way the dog is driving them. More often, it is just the pressure of being stared at as the dog approaches the sheep to fetch them to the shepherd; many a dog would much rather face sheep tails and push from behind.

In training dogs to overcome their fear and build confidence, the trainer will shorten the distance between the sheep and the master. So, the dog uses the handler's presence to boost its confidence like an *umbilical cord* of sorts. Over time and with lots of patience, the trainer and master can extend the distance the dog is asked to work as its confidence builds.

We too feel more confident with the Father and our Savior right there beside us, urging us on to develop the gifts and skills He has equipped us with. Sometimes we feel He's asking too much, but we love Him and truly want to please Him. So, we keep trying. I believe that confidence in our case represents the boldness we are to have in proclaiming the gospel, not just to look at people but to share the good news with passion. Knowing that He is ever-present on the sheep field, better yet giving us guidance through His Spirit, we can not only complete the task but be correct in the path we take. I love how David expresses his desire to serve the Master and recognizes God will give him what is needed. Read what he says in the following psalm. "Restore to me the joy of your salvation and grant me a willing spirit, to sustain me" (Ps. 51:12 NIV). This was such an important lesson the Holy Spirit inspired several writers to reinforce it. In Proverbs 3:26, "For the LORD will be your confidence and will keep your foot from being snared" (NIV). And again in Isaiah 32:17, "The fruit of righteousness will be peace; the effect of righteousness will be quietness and confidence forever" (NIV).

Corrections

These words and phrases are *growled at the dog* to correct the unwanted behavior.

1. Hey
2. Listen/Listen to Me
3. Get Back
4. Not those, These
5. Get out of that!

6. What are you doing in here?

7. Knock it off!

8. You just lost your sheep!

Often when I correct the dogs with these phrases – I hear those same words ringing in my ears from the Spirit, especially the "**Listen to Me.**"

Everyone wants a well-trained dog. Biddable, obedient, and respectful, but not everyone is willing to love the dog enough to put in the time. Training and discipline take time; there is no quick and easy "fix." Having a good sheepdog means having a relationship with the dog.

Tough love is fair, reasonable, and the demonstration of unconditional love. The dog will follow the commands and direction because it wants to please the master more than anything. They learn that disobedience will separate them from the master.

Questions to Ponder

1. Have you ever found yourself running amuck? What circumstance drove your actions? When you realized what you had done, how did you feel?

    _____

    _____

2. Are you willing to use the gifts God endowed you with? When you are using your gifts in His service, how do you feel? Are there gifts you have that you are not using for God? If so, what is holding you back?

    _____

    _____

3. Do you ever feel that you would rather engage in disgusting behaviors than stretch yourself outside of the comfort zone?

    _____

    _____

4. Do you find yourself pouting when the Master asks you to do something? Do you pout if the service He is requiring of you is not what you want? Is it the people He is asking you to serve that causes your hesitancy?

    _____

    _____

CHAPTER 7

CALLED TO OBEY

Call to Obey

When sheepdogs do wrong, take the wrong direction, or come in too tight or too fast, they are told to lie down and listen. Sometimes they dig in their heels and refuse to listen, turning the training session into a battle of wills. In those instances, the trainer may use a snapper stick, which has a leather flap on the end that makes a loud pop when slapped on the ground to get their attention.

They must learn there is no room for willful disobedience. Disobedient dogs find themselves locked up in crates or kennels, isolated from others and, more importantly, the master. Restricting freedom helps dogs recognize the shepherd is in charge. We too suffer consequences for disobedience.

Time in isolation gives them time to think, and border collies DO think! In fact, any time we are training a difficult skill, when the dog tries to comply and is successful in the exercise, we always stop there to give them something to think about. It is uncanny, but my dogs almost always have more success and obedience in the second training session than the first. It is obvious they have thought about what is expected, what went wrong, and what they can do to make it right.

When I tell them, "You did good today!" or "Good listening, good work today!" it revs them up. They are delighted with the opportunity to please me and be praised for their efforts. Obedience has the reward of more opportunities to work sheep, play time with other dogs in the pack, and, best of all, time with the master.

Tough Love

No one wants to be in trouble, but sometimes we bring it on ourselves. If we have the audacity to try to manipulate God, we will experience tough love. Jonah is a prime example of God's discipline. Jonah tried to beg off from what God was asking him, and physically tried to run and hide from God. We can all see how stupid this is when we consider the story of Jonah. But sometimes we are guilty of the same foolishness. Heed the warning of the Hebrew writer:

> My son, do not make light of the LORD's discipline, and do not lose heart when he rebukes you, because the LORD disciplines those he loves, and he punishes everyone he accepts as a son. Endure hardship as discipline; God is treating you as sons, for what son is not disciplined by his father? (Hebrews 12:5-7 NIV)

LESSON 14

Obedience is not <u>optional.</u> It is a prerequisite to God's <u>promise</u>, rest, and protection.

Wait for Direction

Border collies quickly learn there is a pattern for everything; not only in the daily routine of farm life, but also in competition at the sheep dog trials. Even though they generally know what to expect, they must wait for the master or handler's direction.

When they step onto the field, they are to look or scan for the sheep to spot their whereabouts, but wait for the command. The master always knows:

- where the sheep are
- pitfalls in the terrain or course
- problem areas, distractions, and the draw
- the type of sheep and the pressure they respond to
- which dog they are sending to work, *knowing what that dog needs to be successful.*

Once the dog has been sent, it must continue to check that the sheep are in the same place. The dog needs to come in quietly and methodically behind the sheep to lift or move them forward. The dog must always be aware of the master's presence so they can bring the sheep directly to the master without detours.

The border collie can work independently once given directions, but many prefer to have "contact" with the master. Contact can be a soft whistle or words gently spoken. Once the job is done, the dog waits to hear "That'll do" and "Go to water." There is always praise for a job well done and delight back with the master.

In our case, there is no doubt that the Master is well aware of the course set before us. He knows the terrain, how rugged the climb will be. He knows our strengths and weaknesses. He has provided every opportunity for us to be successful. He watches us every step of the way, gently guiding us home. There is never a question of His presence. If we listen, we can hear the soft whisper of His Spirit in our souls. Following His direction for our lives, we will experience His joy and His peace – there is nothing better.

Paul writes, "Formerly he was useless to you, but now he has become useful both to you and to me" (Philem. 1:11 NIV). I love how the psalmist puts it, "I run in the path of your commands, for you have set my heart free. ...Direct me in the path of your commands, for there I find delight" (Ps. 119:32, 35 NIV).

LESSON 15

There is no substitute for <u>obedience</u> and no greater delight than to <u>submit</u> to the Master's will – if you know the <u>Master</u>.

Learn by Example

Border collies can learn a lot by watching each other work. They take note of the way the sheep move and what seems to be successful for that dog on those sheep.

Like we talked about, there are ten commands, each with a specific whistle. Generally, whistles are introduced after the dog in training has been responding correctly to voice commands. They are taught one or two whistles at a time with lots of repetition and reinforcement.

Once a dog is "on whistles," he will be able to know from the first note or tone of the whistle:

1. To stop or keep going
2. The pace to move the sheep
3. Which direction to go or turn
4. When the task is done.

Whenever I worked Junebug, Rascal was always present. After working Junebug, it was her turn. One day, out of habit from working with Junebug, I gave Rascal a whistle command and she took it. I gave another and she took that too. To my surprise, Rascal actually learned all my whistles by watching me work Junebug. She is a very smart dog, and Junebug is a good example of an obedient sheepdog. Many a trainer uses an experienced older dog to demonstrate and teach younger dogs. It is amazing to me how much they can learn by watching.

God is so awesome; in His infinite wisdom, He took advantage of the fact that we are always watching each other. He admonishes the older to teach the younger and to be careful about our example. I have heard it said that folks don't want to hear a message; they want to SEE it!

Jesus tells the disciples:

> I have set you an example that you should do as I have done for you. I tell you the truth, no servant is greater than his master, nor is a messenger greater than the one who sent him. Now that you know these things, you will be blessed if you do them (John 13:15-17 NIV).

Paul encouraged Timothy to be a good example. As he writes in 1 Timothy 4:12, 14-15 (NIV):

> Don't let anyone look down on you because you are young, but set an example for the believers in speech, in life, in love, in faith and purity. ... Do not neglect your gift,...Be diligent in these matters; give yourself wholly to them, so that everyone may see your progress.

Blind Outrun I Can't Find My Sheep!?!

From day one of sheepherding training, the dog is always taught to look for the sheep and to keep them in sight. It is imperative that when the dog is sent to get sheep:

1) sheep are on the field somewhere,
2) that the dog spot the sheep and keep checking their position,
3) or, in the case of a blind outrun, they go out looking out until they find them.

At short distances, sheep are easily seen, and the dog has no trouble spotting them; *up to 200 yards away in herding is considered a short distance.* It is important that dogs be sent for sheep at greater and greater distances to stretch them out. Otherwise, the dog will go about 200 yards and turn in looking for them rather than looking out, back behind them. The master needs to know where the sheep are so they can direct or redirect the dog to them. Once a dog is sent and cannot find the sheep, they go into a panic or at least become anxious. They know they are expected to find sheep. It is the task they have been given and equipped to do.

Rascal was able to spot her sheep at the first dog trial at a distance of 325 yards, and she went out with confidence to gather them and bring them to my feet. Her second and third dog trials were blind outruns. We had worked on looking for the sheep before going to those trials, but the training field maxed out at 215 yards, so she was looking inside that trajectory. I stopped her when she started turning in at the usual place for a 200-yard outrun and gave her the redirect to look back. She looked back, cast out some, and started back in. I gave her another redirect, but she was now in panic mode, running back and forth, looking who knows where and trying desperately to find her sheep.

I left the post and went running toward her to calm her down and lead her to the sheep. But she was so frenzied, she would not lie down and wait for me; she just kept running. At that point, the only thing to do was to get her off the field.

The next day was the same thing; however, I told her I would help her find the sheep if she would just trust me. As she started her frenzy, I was already down the field even with her, and I called her to me. She came but she kept looking this way and that. When she got close to me, I told her to lie down and look back. She did but not far enough. Again, I told her to look back and pointed at them. She saw them and started running out to get them, casting out as she got closer. She brought them to me and we walked them off the field together. I knew that the next trial would not be blind outruns, and so we practiced with the sheep visible. What I did not realize is that the tension of not finding her sheep was still there in her mind.

The next trial the sheep were visible, but at a distance of 375 yards. I sent her and she took off with a nice wide arc; and if she had stayed on that trajectory, she would have found her sheep. But she turned in, and it was panic city all over again. I ran out to her to calm her down and lead her to the sheep. She was so panicked, I had to call her to my feet and pet her calmly. I walked her out, telling her to look; then she saw them and took off. But her anxiety was so strong that she blasted into them and sent them scurrying in all different directions. I called her back and resent her; she brought them to me, and we lead them off the field. It was then I noticed that not only was her jaw quivering, but her teeth were chattering. She was a mess because she was not successful on her own, and now the anxiety of just going out to get sheep was intense. The psalmist reminds us to put our trust in the Shepherd. Psalm 33:20-22 says: "We wait in hope for the LORD; he is our help and our shield. In him our hearts rejoice, for we trust in his holy name. May your unfailing love rest upon us, O LORD, even as we put our hope in you" (NIV).

Encouragement

I spent the next week at bigger fields hiding sheep and walking her out to them until she found them. Each time she found them, I praised her fervently and pet her calmly. By the end of the week, she seemed to be feeling much more confident. Better yet, she was also looking out as she was sent. I told her repeatedly on the way to the trial and at the trial, "You're going find your sheep! If you have trouble, I promise to come help."

When I sent her out at the next trial, she ran out strong and confident – she found her sheep at 350 yards and brought them straight to my feet. The rest of the course wasn't that great, but she found them. I was ready to leave the post to help her, and I believe she knew that I would.

Rascal, when she is happy and excited, will come up and stand on her hind legs into my outstretched arms – like we're dancing. Since that trial, she has been working really hard to follow my commands to the letter. She's giving it all she's got. Needless to say, our time with the sheep is now a joy; she is becoming a very nice sheepdog. My trainer was not too sure that Rascal would work out in the beginning; she told me not to get my hopes up. Now she says that Rascal and I are quite a team. She is pleased with how she's turned around.

Like me, Rascal had to find herself at the love and mercy of the master. I knew if she would just try, she could become a good sheepdog. She had to know that I believed in her, that I would help her; there would be tough love when needed but lots of joy and delight when she rose to my expectations.

We have a Master and a Shepherd that wants nothing more than for us to succeed. He wants us to trust Him, even when we cannot see where we are going. Talk about a blind outrun; only God knows where we are headed. We know He only sends us when there is work to be done. He is there in the field with us, helping us every step of the way. He knows when we are trying: when we need more training, more practice, and much more time in His presence. There is nothing sweeter than knowing that God wants us to experience delight and joy in full, faithful obedience to His call.

Do you ever feel as if you are running in circles? You know you have a job to do, but for the life of you, you cannot figure out where to start or how to begin? When we are frantic, we are of no use to anyone. In that frame of mind, it is just about impossible to hear the still, small whisper of the Lord or His Spirit. When I'm in a frenzy running here and there, I need to listen for His call. When He calls my name, I know if I go straight to Him, He will help. He will comfort me, and, best of all, He loves me enough to discipline whenever necessary.

The following verses comfort me when I am unsure or discouraged. Romans 15:5-6: "May the God who gives endurance and encouragement give you a spirit of unity among yourselves as you follow Christ Jesus, so that with one heart and mouth you may glorify the God and Father of our LORD Jesus Christ" (NIV). Psalm 10:17 (NIV): "You hear, O LORD, the desire of the afflicted; you encourage them and you listen to their cry."

Stop and listen for Him--He is calling us to be still.

When we listen, we will act wisely: "He who answers before listening – that is his folly and his shame" (Prov. 18:13 NIV). And we will learn, Proverbs 18:15: "The heart of the discerning acquires knowledge; the ears of the wise seek it out" (NIV).

Stand still and watch: "Moses answered the people, 'Do not be afraid. Stand firm and you will see the deliverance the Lord will bring you today. The Egyptians you see today you will never see again. The Lord will fight for you; you need only to be still'" (Exod. 14:13-14 NIV).

The people were hostile and despairing, but Moses encouraged them to watch the powerful way God would rescue them. Moses had the right perspective. It looked hopeless with certain death, so Moses called on God to thwart the enemy's plan. Although we are not being chased by an army, we can still feel trapped in a corner with no escape. Rather than sink into depression, we need to embrace the fortitude of Moses standing firm – to see God's deliverance.

At the Master's Side

Don't let anything hinder you from being at the Master's side. Rest comfortably in His will and His presence. The following verses can bring comfort when you know the Master and seek His will. Psalm 139:1-5 (NIV):

> O LORD, you have searched me and you know me. You know when I sit and when I rise; you perceive my thoughts from afar. You discern my going out and my lying down; you are familiar with all my ways. Before a word is on my tongue you know it completely, O LORD.

> You hem me in – behind and before; you have
> laid your hand upon me.

Micah 6:8: "He has showed you, O man, what is good. And what does the LORD require of you? To act justly and to love mercy and to walk humbly with your God" (NIV). I love the charge Joshua gave to his fellow Israelites as they went to their home across the Jordan. "But be very careful to keep the commandment and the law that Moses the servant of the LORD gave you: to love the LORD your God, to walk in all his ways, to obey his commands, to hold fast to him and to serve him with all your heart and all your soul" (Joshua 22:5 NIV).

Transformed and Growing

Over time, Rascal has become a sheepdog. She learned the relationship with the shepherd is second to none. She now realizes that I love her and want her to be the best she can be. We spend lots of time in the field together working sheep, practicing new skills, and enjoying each other's company. She has come to know that obedience means the master is pleased, which results in praise, encouragement, and, most of all, attention. She still has her sulky, pouty moments, but they are fewer and farther between. She is young yet, so there will be lots more learning and growing to be the best sheepdog she can be. But I can say that she seems to have caught my vision for her on some level and is striving to please.

I couldn't have been prouder at our last sheep dog trial in Helotes. It was a whole different experience for her. Working in an arena instead of a 20+ acre field, she was required to work quietly and steadily to move some very difficult sheep. She did what I asked of her, and I was very happy with her performance and workmanship. We had quite a few comments from our peers about how good she was and that we are becoming quite the team. Thankfully, my granddaughter Alyssa was there and filmed the run.

Now a Sheepdog

No matter how far we come, sin is always within reach. Rascal provided an excellent example for this point. One day we had a wonderful practice. She was listening, responsive, obedient, and successful in the tasks I asked of her. As a reward, I allowed her to move a flock of about thirty-five sheep to the "back 40" acres in a pasture by the stock tank to graze. She loved it! It was different and driving a group that big, she felt the power. She was so delighted with herself once they were safely secured in that pasture; her eyes sparkled, and she came running up to me to "dance." I praised her for the work. Then as the other shepherd and I walked the fence line of her property, Rascal would run ahead a bit, look back for me, and come running back to my side.

At one point, she was a short distance ahead sniffing and then dropped to the ground to roll. She rolled and rolled. When she got up, she was covered in fresh cow manure. Some of those disgusting habits of rolling in muck are still very much ingrained. She did not appreciate being hosed down to clean her up, but I told her she'd have to be clean if she wanted to be with me.

That is exactly what the Master has done for us. We must be clean and washed with the blood of our Savior to be in His presence. Clearly, no matter how far we come, sin calls us back to wallow in the muck. I am so thankful that Jesus' blood is always available to cleanse me from my sin every time I fail. The Shepherd never gives up on us, even if we give up on ourselves. He will give us all the help and training we need to be successful in His service. When we succeed, He is thrilled with our progress. He loves us and calls us His own and His children. That relationship far exceeds that of a shepherd and a sheepdog.

Questions to Ponder

1. Have you ever begun a service or ministry and decided it was not what you thought or wanted to do? Did you think about quitting or did you continue, but your heart wasn't in it?

   _____

   _____

2. Do you beg God not to make life so hard; do you find yourself throwing up your hands or pouting? Have you gone so far as to beg God to come quickly?

   _____

   _____

3. Can you think of a time that God used tough love with you? Did you realize what He was doing at the time?

   _____

   _____

4. Do you still find yourself wallowing in the muck of sin, rather than striving to be holy like the Shepherd? What gets you off track? What steps have you taken to lessen that behavior?

   _____

   _____

CHAPTER 8
DIFFICULT PATHS

Proverbs 19:21: "Many are the plans in a man's heart, but it is the LORD's purpose that prevails."

A fellow handler's dog named Joe had an encounter with a vehicle. In Texas, there was a huge sheep farm approximately 1,000 head or more. The highway cut through their property. Consequently, from time to time, it was necessary to take the sheep across the highway to the other side. One day, Joe was herding the flock across the highway. Sheep covered a fair piece of the road. Unfortunately, there was a car apparently in a hurry to get somewhere and once the sheep started moving off the road, the driver sped up and ran over Joe. The driver told the owner he never saw the dog, just the sheep. Wow! Am I the only one who sees the irony in that? The shepherd put Joe's lifeless body in the truck. They got the sheep put up and drove to the vet. On the way, Joe came to and out of shock. Two vets checked him over and said they could find nothing wrong. Joe's story has a happy ending; he continued herding and died of old age at fifteen.

Daunting Task

Have you ever taken a long look at the size of the task ahead, wondering how on earth you will ever be able to do the work, much less complete it? The good news is you are not alone. Even when there are no others in sight for that particular mission or ministry, God, the perfect Shepherd, is right there beside us. In fact, He is going before us; we just need to follow in His footsteps wherever they lead, knowing He is big enough for the task. And He will equip you for what you need, for each and every task He sends you to. I love the song the children sing, "My God is So Big," because if you believe the premise of that song, you won't shy away from the work or the path to which you have been called.

I am reminded of the struggle Elijah faced when he feared he was alone and frustrated that there was no end in sight or help from men or God. Read what he said in 1 Kings 19:10-15, 18 (NIV):

> He replied, "I have been very zealous for the LORD God Almighty. The Israelites have rejected your covenant, broken down your altars and put your prophets to death with the sword. I am the only one left, and now they are trying to kill me too."

> The Lord said, "Go out and stand on the mountain in the presence of the LORD; for the LORD is about to pass by."

> Then a great and powerful wind tore the mountains apart and shattered the rocks before the LORD, but the LORD was not in the wind.

After the wind there was an earthquake, but the LORD was not in the earthquake. After the earthquake came a fire, but the LORD was not in the fire. And after the fire came a gentle whisper. When Elijah heard it he pulled his cloak over his face, and went out and stood at the mouth of the cave. Then a voice said to him, "What are you doing here, Elijah?"

He replied, "I have been very zealous for the LORD God Almighty. The Israelites have rejected your covenant, broken down your altars, and put your prophets to death with the sword. I am the only one left, and now they are trying to kill me too."

The LORD said to him … "Yet I reserve seven thousand in Israel—all whose knees have not bowed down to Baal and all whose mouths have not kissed him."

God responded by letting Elijah witness His glory and talking directly to Him. He told Elijah of all the Israelites that were standing with God and would be standing with Elijah. Better yet, knowing how vulnerable Elijah felt, God provided him with a companion, Elisha, to work with him side by side. Our God knows us like no other; He is very aware of our need for others, for help. So, when the going gets tough, He often provides someone we can see and feel to share the Master's touch upon our hearts and lives.

After Elijah was taken up into heaven, Elisha continued the work God gave him. Elisha knew He had a big God. I have always loved Elisha for his faith and his graciousness, allowing his servant to see God at work. This is my favorite story of Elisha:

> When the servant of the man of God got up and went out early the next morning, an army with horses and chariots had surrounded the city. "Oh, my lord, what shall we do?" the servant asked. "Don't be afraid," the prophet answered. "Those who are with us are more than those who are with them." And Elisha prayed, "O LORD, open his eyes so he may see." Then the LORD opened the servant's eyes, and he looked and saw the hills full of horses and chariots of fire all around Elisha (2 Kings 6:15-17 NIV).

LESSON 16

The Shepherd is <u>big enough</u> to aid you in the task and He goes <u>before you</u>.

Climb the Mountain

On the mountaintop, God shares His beauty, His majesty, and shows us His glory. He does not meet with us face to face, like He did with Moses, or talk to us personally, like He did with Elijah. Yet you cannot help but feel His presence.

Everyone loves the mountaintop experience, but you can't get there without climbing the mountain. The rugged climb and journey to get there is not always pleasant. It can be rough; you can get scraped up or lost along the way. No matter how difficult the path, if you look up, the peak is always in sight. And you can know without a doubt that God will provide whatever you need for the journey.

Look again at the story of Elijah, from 1 Kings 19:3-9 (NIV):

> Elijah was afraid and ran for his life. When he came to Beersheba in Judah, he left his servant there, while he himself went a day's journey into the desert. He came to a broom tree, sat down under it and prayed that he might die. "I have had enough, LORD," he said. "Take my life; I am no better than my ancestors."

Then he lay down under the tree and fell asleep. All at once an angel touched him and said, "Get up and eat."

He looked around and there by his head was a cake of bread baked over hot coals and a jar of water. He ate and drank and then lay down again.

The angel of the LORD came back a second time and touched him and said, "Get up and eat, for the journey is too much for you."

So he got up and ate and drank. Strengthened by that food he traveled forty days and forty nights until he reached Horeb, the mountain of God. There he went into a cave and spent the night."

Note: it was not a short climb. It required him to travel forty days and forty nights to get there.

Take on the Ram

God did not remove the challenges and dangers for the prophet Elijah in his service; he had to face them head on. The same is true with a stock dog. They are sent into the field, knowing that they can face an angry ram or even a bull, in order to follow the master's command. I am sure based on their relative size the dogs feel like they are battling Goliath. Yet, they are willing to face the danger because of their love for the master.

Just remember that you are never alone, and He will give you the strength to complete the task or the journey. As God told Joshua, "No one will be able to stand up against you all the days of your life. As I was with Moses, so I will be with you; I will never leave you nor forsake you" (Josh. 1:5 NIV). Peter reminds us in 1 Peter 4:11, "If anyone speaks, he should do it as one speaking the very words of God. If anyone serves, he should do it with the strength God provides, so that in all things God may be praised through Jesus Christ. To him be the glory and the power for ever and ever. Amen" (NIV). And Jesus taught us in the Sermon on the Mount from Matthew 6: 6, 8, 31-32:

> But when you pray, go into your room, close the door, and pray to your Father, who is unseen. Then your Father, who sees what is done in secret, will reward you. ...Do not be like them, for your Father knows what you need before you ask him.
>
> So do not worry, saying, 'What shall we eat?' or 'What shall we drink?'
>
> or What shall we wear?' For the pagans run after all these things, and your heavenly Father knows that you need them (NIV).

LESSON 17

The Master always <u>knows</u> and <u>provides</u> what you need.

Uphill Battle

Sometimes the work and the journey is so hard and precarious it feels like we are pushing a boulder up the hill. It feels that any moment we can be crushed if we falter or lose our grip. Why does it have to be uphill? Why not a smooth plain, or at least downhill, so we can rest? I recently heard a quote by singer Wintley Phipps, "Son if the mountain were smooth, you couldn't climb it" (https://www.ele-phant journal.com).

There is a lot of truth in that statement. We need the rough terrain for something to grasp and to get a foothold. Remember, we want the mountaintop, and it is always uphill from the valley. God provides some plateaus along the way for a bit of respite, but you are still out on a ledge as it were.

Challenge

For the dogs, nothing about sheepherding is easy. There are always obstacles along the way – sheep that do not want to move, terrain that is difficult to climb, etc. Sometimes there are unseen challenges, such as caved in mole hills and tunnels. The dog must love the master and have a passion for the work to rise to the challenge every time he is sent. Dogs do not set their schedules; there are no days off. When they are called, they are expected to come and work until the task is complete. In rough terrain and rolling hills covered with brush, it is not uncommon for the dog to be working some distance from the shepherd. The shepherd must have faith in the dog that it will continue the work, even though the master is out of sight. The dog must trust the master completely, that he knows what he is doing and that the dog has the skills to complete the task. It must also believe that the master will come to its aid when needed, to share in the work and to encourage the dog.

We too have challenges and mountains to move. Thankfully, Jesus provided a way for us to move them: Faith in Him. There can be no greater Master or Shepherd than the Lord Himself. He is ever present in times of trouble.

Elijah had a mountaintop experience, but first a valley of testing, later another mountaintop experience followed by despair. God never left him, even when he felt alone – his faith in God brought him through the valley no matter the danger. His faith was challenged when the brook dried up, but he continued to serve the Master. He put himself in harm's way, meeting with King Ahab before the showdown; he was vulnerable but never without God. Let us flashback to the valley of testing. Read 1 Kings 17:1-7:

> Now Elijah the Tishbite, from Tishbe in Gilead, said to Ahab, "As the LORD, the God of Israel, lives, whom I serve, there will be neither dew nor rain in the next few years except at my word." Then the word of the LORD came to Elijah: "Leave here, turn eastward and hide in the Kerith Ravine, east of the Jordan. You will drink from the brook, and I have ordered the

ravens to feed you there." So he did what the LORD had told him. He went to Kerith Ravine, east of the Jordan, and stayed there. The ravens brought him bread and meat in the evening, and he drank from the brook. Sometime later the brook dried up because there had been no rain in the land (NIV).

The Showdown on Mount Carmel

You know the story from **1 *Kings 18:19-42***: one mountain **(v 19)**, two bulls **(v 23)**, two altars **(v 26 & v 30)**, people waiting to see the outcome before they would commit **(v 24)**. Baal, of course, did nothing **(v 26)**, and God, of course, did everything and then some **(v 38)**, and the people fell down and worshiped the Lord, the one true God **(v 39)**. God's people killed the prophets of Baal **(v 40)**. Elijah climbed the mountain to pray for rain **(v 42)**. And the rains came! You know what happened next, we opened with those verses.

Claim the promises in the following verses:

Psalm 46:1-3: "God is our refuge and strength, an ever –present help in trouble. Therefore we will not fear, though the earth give way and the mountains fall into the heart of the sea, though its waters roar and foam and the mountains quake with their surging" (NIV).

Isaiah 44: 2: "This is what the LORD says – he who made you, who formed you in the womb, and who will help you: Do not be afraid, O Jacob, my servant, Jeshurun, whom I have chosen" (NIV).

Isaiah 46: 3-4: "Listen to me, O house of Jacob, all you who remain of the house of Israel, you whom I have upheld since you were conceived, and have carried since your birth. Even to your old age and gray hairs I am he, I am he who will sustain you. I have made you and I will carry you; I will sustain you and I will rescue you" (NIV).

John 16:33: "I have told you these things, so that in me you may have peace. In this world you will have trouble. But take heart! I have overcome the world" (NIV).

I will never forget back in the eighties, Kip and I were studying with a young couple who was hesitating to make a commitment to the Lord. An elder in the church joined us in the study. He told them, "If you give your life to God, you will have trouble, **but you will also have God.**" I remember thinking, *What are you doing? Now they will never obey the gospel.* But they did. If you love the Lord, having Him beside you is paramount to anything.

LESSON 18

The Master is always <u>available</u> and <u>present</u>.

Stand Your Ground

When a dog is challenged by a ewe, threatening to head butt the dog or "drill them into the ground," the safest thing to do is to stand their ground. If they make the mistake of turning away or moving backward, the sheep will recognize that as a weakness and they are more likely to be charged. As we have seen in the previous lessons, it is hard to stand your ground, especially if they've hurt you in the past. The dog must exude confidence, even if it is anxious inside. The mark of a true, faithful sheepdog is one that will never give in or take the easy way out.

In these days where we read and see persecution in areas all around the world, we must know that at some point, Christian persecution will be a threat here in the United States. I must admit that I am really a coward, especially when it comes to pain from an outside attack. The thought of facing such persecution gives me goosebumps. I am praying fervently that in the event that I am faced with such, I will stand my ground, claiming Jesus as my Savior no matter the cost. I want to have the courage of Shadrach, Meshach, and Abednego from *Daniel 3:16-18* that even if God doesn't rescue me from certain death, I will not serve or worship another god or idol. At the very least, I want to be convicted as a believer and a child of God.

When King Jehoshaphat and those living in Judah and Jerusalem were threatened by an enemy army, God put His words in the mouth of a Levite to share with his king and brothers. Read what God told them in 2 Chronicles 20:17 (NIV): "You will not have to fight this battle. Take up your positions; **stand firm** and **see the deliverance the Lord will give you**, O Judah and Jerusalem. Do not be afraid; do not be discouraged. **Go out to face them tomorrow, and the Lord will be with you**" *(emphasis mine)*.

Driven

Understand that this is an intense amount of pressure to put on a dog. The slow, methodical training developed faith and confidence in the master's direction; now the dog will be able to accept such a challenge. Two things to remember: When given the challenge, the master is *ALWAYS nearby and watching,* and the master will help, guide, and direct the dog through to success. Once the task is done, the master will call the dog to his side and lavish him with praise and affection. The dog will readily take on the challenge again in the future because of the relationship with the master.

Sometimes we are in difficult situations because we are being tested. If we pass the test, we are then able to serve. Look at the story of David; even to his family, he was insignificant and just a shepherd boy, but God had a plan. First Samuel 16:12-13, 19 (NIV):

> So he sent and had him brought in. He was ruddy, with a fine appearance and handsome features. Then the LORD said, "Rise and anoint him; he is the one." So Samuel took the horn of oil and anointed him in the presence of his brothers, and from that day on the Spirit of the LORD came upon David in power. ...Then Saul sent messengers to Jesse and said, "Send me your son David, who is with the sheep."

He was anointed king in front of his father and his brothers, and then sent back to tend his father's sheep. The story continues in 1 Samuel 17:14-15, 20:

> David was the youngest. The three oldest followed Saul, but David went back and forth from Saul to tend his father's sheep at Bethlehem. ...Early in the morning David left the flock with a shepherd, loaded up and set

out, as Jesse directed. He reached the camp as the army was going out to its battle positions, shouting the war cry (NIV).

He passed the test, so now a call to service. Listen to his passion as he talks to King Saul in 1 Samuel 17:32, 34, 37 (NIV):

> David said to Saul, "Let no one lose heart on account of this Philistine; your servant will go and fight him." But David said to Saul, "Your servant has been keeping his father's sheep. When a lion or a bear came and carried off a sheep from the flock, I went after it, struck it and rescued the sheep from its mouth. …The LORD who delivered me from the paw of the lion and the paw of the bear will deliver me from the hand of this Philistine."

We all know the story; David indeed served his God and his people. We also know that he was tested time and time again, and he served the Lord like no other. I believe David understood the relationship of the Shepherd to His sheep better than anyone. That may be the very reason he was called a man after God's own heart.

LESSON 19

The first call is a <u>test</u>; the next is to <u>service</u>.

Questions to Ponder

1. Consider a time when you had a daunting task in your service to the Lord. What did you learn from your experience?

   _____

   _____

2. Consider a time when you felt like you had to take on the ram. Did you feel alone like Elijah? What happened?

   _____

   _____

3. What do you think about the future of persecution here in America? How are you preparing yourself and your family to withstand the risks and dangers ahead as you serve the Lord?

   _____

   _____

4. Consider a time when you were tested. How did it apply to your service to follow that experience?

_____

_____

CHAPTER 9

HEARTACHE

Snakebite – Proactive Prevention

An ounce of prevention is worth a pound of cure, or so they say. At any rate, annually in March before the snakes come out of hibernation, Junebug, Rascal, and Tux get their rattlesnake vaccination. The vaccine was created to protect dogs in the event of a rattlesnake bite; happily, the makers of the vaccine have found that there is enough similarity in the venom that the vaccine also protects in the event of a bite from a copperhead or water moccasin. Without the vaccine, the dog has little to no chance even with the anti-venom, which must be specific to the snake and at cost of $1000-$1500 per injection. If a dog has been vaccinated, treatment generally requires only antihistamine and possibly steroids. Rattlesnake vaccines must be given annually to maintain the dog's antibody level to counter the viper's venom; otherwise, the bite is often fatal.

We too need to constantly boost our spiritual immunity with regular feedings on the Word and dependence on the Holy Spirit.

Sometimes people focus on the cost rather than the benefit or fall into the trap of, "It won't happen to me; I'm a good person." However, the cost of the vaccine or following Christ is cheaper in the long run. We have the absolute perfect anti-venom available to us through the blood of Jesus. His life-giving power in the blood will remove any vile toxins from sin and Satan over and over again, if we just ask and trust Him to do so. Thank God we have such a cleansing, healing source just a prayer away.

Junebug's story

During vacation one summer, I received a text that Junebug had been bitten by something, probably a copperhead, and that she was quite swollen. My friend Pearl had already begun giving her Benadryl every few hours and was keeping her quiet in a crate. Junebug was only let out to relieve herself. It was scary to think how vulnerable Junebug was at that moment; however, I knew she was in good hands. Pearl has had a lot of experience in caring for dogs with snakebite. She knows the signs, the treatment, and remains calm and vigilant in their care. In my mind, I knew that Junebug was protected because she had had the rattlesnake vaccine and now only required antihistamine and possibly steroids or antibiotics to prevent an infection at the wound site.

Yet, my heart kept ruminating over the more negative possibilities; I could not seem to get those frightening images out of my head. I prayed for her healing and thanked God that she was getting care with Pearl. Pearl let me know that she had taken her to the vet because there was still a lot of swelling. The vet gave her a stronger antihistamine and steroid antibiotics. By the time I saw her, there was still some swelling of her lip, and her throat looked like she had a small goiter. She was going stir crazy being crated and anxiously wanted to be out working sheep. In fact, once she started feeling better and the swelling started receding, she did not appreciate being cooped up in the crate. It was for her own good, but she saw it as a punishment. I am left to wonder if there will be a memory, a lesson learned to avoid snakes in general; to have a healthy respect for the danger they present.

I hasten to point out that the dogs are not seeking danger or snakebites but instead are playing or working in the field where snakes are present. Snakes are always present in the field, not always visible but present even when hibernating. The difference with Satan is that he does not hibernate, and he is seeking to devour us. Knowing that, how can we depend on milk lessons from the Word, a trauma-based prayer life, lack of worship or any combination of the three?

Unfortunately, as humans we tend to be grumblers; I must admit I've done my share of complaining to God. The Israelites were no better, even with the visible cloud by day and the cloud of fire by night, showing God's very presence. God got their attention in the desert with the snakes.

As you read in Numbers 21:4-6,

> They traveled from Mount Hor along the route to the Red Sea, to go around Edom. But the people grew impatient on the way; they spoke against God and against Moses and said, "Why have you brought us up out of Egypt to die in the desert? There is no bread! There is no water! And we detest this miserable food!" Then the LORD sent venomous snakes among them; they bit the people and many Israelites died (NIV).

God made a way, as He always does, for healing and salvation. Look at Numbers 21:7-9:

> The people came to Moses and said, "We sinned when we spoke against the LORD and against you. Pray that the LORD will take the **snakes** away from us." So Moses prayed for the people. The LORD said to Moses, "Make a **snake** and put it up on a pole; anyone who is **bitten** can look at it and live." So Moses made a bronze snake and put it up on a pole. Then when anyone was bitten by a **snake** and looked at the bronze **snake**, he lived (NIV).

Jesus refers to that story in John 3:14-15, as foreshadowing of His sacrifice for us. "Just as Moses lifted up the **snake** in the desert, so the Son of Man must be lifted up, that everyone who believes in him may have eternal life" (NIV).

Bronze Serpent

I cannot help but think that I've responded the same way when God has allowed something or someone to take a bite out of my complacency or pleasure. I get a swelled head because I get puffed up about the unfairness of the situation, and the last thing I want to do is sit quietly, contained, and wait… and wait… and wait. Thankfully, God has given me everything I need to heal, to change, to overcome the negative effects of the situation. Now if I take the time He's given me to recoup, I'll be all the better for it. Will I remember what God has done for me yet again? Will I learn the lesson I was intended to learn? Will I be more wary of the cunning, slithering Satan from here on out? Lord willing, I will respond in the affirmative to all those questions.

God made it clear to us that Satan is against us, against God, and wants us to fail and lose our souls. Satan is audacious enough to challenge God Himself. Why do we think we can outwit him on our own? Look at the following verses:

Genesis 3:1 (NIV): "Now the **serpent** was more crafty than any of the wild animals the LORD God had made. He said to the woman, "Did God really say, 'You must not eat from any tree in the garden?'"

Job 1:7: "The LORD said to Satan, 'Where have you come from?' Satan answered the LORD, 'From roaming through the earth and going back and forth in it'" (NIV).

Ephesians 6:10-11: "Finally, be strong in the LORD and in his mighty power. Put on the full armor of God so that you can take your stand against the devil's schemes" (NIV).

Like the rattlesnake vaccine, we need to put on the armor of Christ and the Spirit of God to protect us from the bite of Satan. When we have succumbed to the vile poison of sin and temptation, we become puffed up with swelled egos to the point that we are unrecognizable. I heard that EGO is an acronym for *easing God out;* how true. Like the vaccine, God did not prevent snakebites, but God provided a way to remove the harmful effects of the venom, if the Israelites looked up at the serpent on the tree for healing once bitten. *Note that them being able to be healed was predicated on utilizing the prescription God prescribed for them!*

Rattlesnake training using live rattlesnakes that have been defanged is available for dogs. But the training requires the use of shock collars that have been wet down to increase the shock effect if the dog stops to sniff at the snake cage. We too need to be alert and aware of Satan's presence in this world; if we do not put on the full armor of God, our sin will indeed come back to bite us.

Paul warns us in Ephesians 6:12-13 (NIV): "For our struggle is not against flesh and blood, but against the rulers, against the authorities, against the powers of this dark world and against the spiritual forces of evil in the heavenly realms. Therefore put on the full armor of God, so that when the day of evil comes, you may be able to stand your ground, and after you have done everything, to stand."

Sometimes I wish I could learn the lessons more quickly and remember what I learned. It seems I must relearn things all too often because I was sniffing around something I shouldn't and then I'm shocked when I get bit. I am thankful that God most often chooses to give us a way to healing rather than a shock to the system; however, I'm also aware that sometimes it is necessary for God to allow us to experience pain to move away from the deadly sin or complacency.

LESSON 20

The <u>Spirit of God</u> works to help you develop anti-venom to ward off the <u>toxic effects</u> of Satan's attacks.

ACL Strain – The injury

In February of 2014, Junebug and I competed for the first time in the Open Ranch class. As a point of reference,

114

the difference between the Ranch class and the Open Ranch class adds distance and, therefore, difficulty. The outrun changes from 150 yards to 325+ yards. We had a great day. Junebug saw the sheep, listened to the whistles, and watched her sheep. We were working great as a team; we got a score, and we were twelfth out of twenty-nine dogs (just two out of the money). I showered her with praise and beamed with pride.

But Junebug was toe-touching instead of walking on all fours; in fact at times, she was "on three legs." We only entered on that particular Saturday, to enable us to be home for church on Sunday; that was a blessing because it was not until Monday that I realized she was injured. When I took her to the vet, he said she had strained her ACL and would need to be out a minimum of six weeks, and referred me to physical therapy.

ACL Recuperation – Therapy

Recuperation meant six weeks crate rest, laser treatments over the course of four weeks, and physical therapy for six weeks consecutively. It also included ice massages after short walks eight to ten minutes and three to five minutes per day exercises on a physio roll, along with "Sit – Stands" *equivalent to squats for us.*

Working border collies need tons of exercise. Just think, she is used to running up to 325 yards to gather sheep in one swoop; yet now she had to sit in the crate all day. Poor Junebug looked so soulful, like she had lost her best friend; like she was being punished, and she thought she did so well. There was no way to make her understand that she was crated for her own good and healing. I could not let her jump, run, or stand on her hind legs. I couldn't allow her

115

to prance, which is her natural gait. She could only walk, and not much of that. Instead of the freedom of the doggie door, she had to be taken out on a leash to keep her "quiet and calm." She went from seeing sheep four to five days a week to seeing none for fifteen weeks. To make matters worse, the last three or four weeks of that period, a new dog, Rascal, had come into our "pack" and she was coming home smelling like sheep several days a week. I knew that Junebug did not understand. She probably thought I was mad at her, although I gave her as much attention and praise as I could to lift her spirits. But her eyes looked at me as if to say, "What did I do?" "What can I do to make it right with you?" "I want to work sheep – WITH YOU again."

Healing

I have had those same thoughts, prayerfully expressed to God when I have found myself "benched" as it were or, worse, in real trouble. In retrospect, it always seems to happen when I am trying my best to be more fervent in my service, more devoted to my studies, and more faithful in my prayer life. I know of course that Satan is creating most of the chaos around me, trying to elicit doubt and dismay. I find myself asking those questions of God, soul-searching to see what I have done or not done. I beg God to open my eyes and let me learn whatever lesson He is trying to teach me, and PLEASE make it quick. Patience is something I will be working on to my dying days I am afraid. I let the pace of life and my desires get the best of me all too often.

Even though Junebug was in a quandary with the future of her life's work, she was a good patient. She was willing and biddable to do whatever we asked. She let the vet, the vet techs, the physical therapist, and me examine the leg, massage it, manipulate it, and work it. In the course of time, the leg healed, and she was cleared to work as long as we took it slow. To begin with, she was just allowed to walk or trot behind the sheep to drive them wherever I instructed her to take them. Later, she was allowed to do small gathers or short outruns to bring the sheep to me and then back to driving.

I know it was hard because she has always been a dog that gives a 100 percent + and works until the job is done. However, she does not police herself well, so I had to limit her activities to allow the leg and her body to build up stamina. She was so eager to be back on the field, she was making every effort to do exactly what I asked and required of her, trying to be as correct as possible and not wanting anything to get her in trouble or "benched" again. I know it was hard for her to come back slowly, while the new dog was getting ample opportunity to work and train before and after Junebug's short sessions.

LESSON 21

When you <u>don't understand</u> what the Master is doing or why, <u>submit</u> to His will; He will make your paths straight.

Eat My Dust

Sometimes, especially in a Texas drought, the field where you are working is more dust and dirt than grass. The dogs moving sheep are breathing in the sand and dust kicked up by the sheep and their own movement. In those circumstances, it is not unusual to see dirt fly when the dog drops to a lie down. Sometimes the amount of dust and sand overwhelms them, and they cough or seem to gag when they get a glob in their mouths. In the big scheme of things, it is just an irritant, but it definitely takes a toll over the long haul. The sheepdog is not only working in the grit, but they are eating dust.

In May of 2012, Junebug and I went to Mountain Air, New Mexico to compete in a sheep dog trial. The first day was picture perfect. But on day two, we woke up to a howling wind and sandstorm. The wind was constant the entire day; it never let up. Depending on the intensity of the wind, we were eating sand. Everyone was wearing hats and caps with earflaps to protect their ears. It was hard to sit and watch because sitting in the wind with the grit in our faces was a major irritant. I remember opening a water bottle to take a drink, and it felt like I was pouring sand in my mouth along with the water. Wow! It gave me a whole new respect for the dog's perspective. Thankfully, we only had one day of sandstorms. Then it was back to the pleasant weather we had from the beginning. Life is full of irritants, but we cannot make them our focus. There is work to be done.

Storms

Many border collies, because of their acute hearing, are afraid of thunderstorms and lightning. It makes sense that it would be scary if they witnessed a storm sitting alone in an outside kennel; but many are afraid that have never been left outside in the storm. Junebug is so fearful that if she needs to go outside and she sees it is raining, she turns around to come back in as if to say, "I think I'll wait." In fact, her fear of storms is so intense that even when she is in the house, sitting right next to me warm and dry, her bottom jaw quivers and her whole body shakes. Her eyes have a fearful look; she will not eat, drink, or play during those times. She is my shadow, stuck to me like glue or hiding in the dark guest bathroom.

However, if I call her to join me to work sheep even in the pouring rain, she will answer the call. I can see her bristle if there is thunder in the distance, but she continues to work until she hears, "That'll do." The only difference I can see in her willingness to trudge through the fear in a storm is that she is with her master. To serve the master, she is willing to face her fear working alongside as needed.

Moses made it clear that our Master and Shepherd is always with us –don't be afraid. See Deuteronomy 31:6, 8 (NIV):

"Be strong and courageous. **Do not be afraid or terrified** because of them, for the LORD your **God goes with you; he will never leave you nor forsake you.**" ... "The LORD himself goes before you and will be with you; he will never **leave** you nor **forsake** you. **Do not be afraid;** do not be discouraged" (NIV *emphasis mine).*

Rainstorms

We do not work during storms often, but we have faced some tough ones together. Side by side, she walks with me in the pouring rain and howling winds; in darkness overcast with thunder rumbling; even in an ice storm with freezing rain and sleet. Never once does she recoil from the call to duty when the master calls. That is faithful: weathering adversity to serve; facing her deepest fears because there is work to do and she's been called. Like I said before – she is my go-to dog.

Sheep may hide in a rain and thunderstorm, under trees or in the brush, any shelter they can find in the field. That means that the simple task of gathering the sheep has become a game of hide and seek – a blind outrun. This time I may or may not know where the sheep are, although I have an idea – so does Junebug. Under these circumstances, there are times when I cannot see Junebug, *a black dog in the dark.* More importantly, she cannot always see me. With strong winds, she may not be able to hear my whistles or my voice. She must trust that I will not leave her alone in the storm. She continues working, believing that I am out there with her and will call her to my side and to shelter once the job is done.

Storms of Life

When we face storms, we too have the Master out there with us, whether we can see or feel His presence. We can know, without a doubt, He is there. He promised He would never leave us alone; He cherishes us too much. So why do I beg for mercy not to go through the storm? I do not want to face my fears or the darkness. I love sunshine and light. Truth be told, I have wasted more time crying out to be relieved of a storm than it took to go through it. When I have been more trusting, I feel His peace. Knowing the Master is with me, I can weather anything. At times like that, I know He is in the thick of it; no matter what, He'll even carry me if necessary.

Knowing it will pass is comforting, maybe not as quickly as it came but it *will pass.* I remember my grandmother always responding with, "This too shall pass," anytime I told her of a struggle or hardship I was experiencing. I have tried to share that with my grandkids to let them know that no matter the sadness or hurt, *it will pass.* Claim the promise of Hebrews 13:6 (NIV): "So we say with confidence, 'The LORD is my helper; I will not be afraid. What can man do to me?'"

Remember nothing lasts forever; emotional pain will lessen with time and no one is worth losing your life. God promised Noah that He would never again flood the earth as before. So we can know the storm will end and there will again be sunshine.

LESSON 22

Answer the call no matter what. The Master is waiting. This too shall pass.

The promise of constant presence made to Jacob in Genesis, as he fled for his life from Esau, is reiterated to us again and again in both the Old and New Testaments. Genesis 28:15: "I am **with** you and will watch over you wherever you go, and I will bring you back to this land. I will not **leave** you until I have done what I have promised you" (NIV). Claim the promise, face your fears, the Lord is near – see Matthew 28:20: "And surely I am with you always, to the very end of the age" (NIV).

Rainbows

The most beautiful and spectacular displays of God's promise and love are the rainbows He paints across the sky after the storm has passed. I like to think of the rainbow as a *"that'll do."* So, I can rest in the warmth of His sunshine, knowing the battle is over for now. I made it through now stronger than before with yet another reason to trust His faithfulness. As you bask in His light, meditate on the fact that He was not only with you during the storm but *in you.* You cannot get any closer than that! Prayerfully, with each storm you battle together, the greater your peace and trust in Him. He is not just a Master, but the Creator of the universe and Master of all.

Questions to Ponder

1. Do you think about Satan as the dangerous viper he is? Are you protected? Does your prayer life focus more on relationship-building with God rather than crisis intervention?

   _____

   _____

2. When God has slowed you down or stopped you with health concerns or other barriers, what thoughts have gone through your mind? Are you thankful for the break or worried about the future?

   _____

   _____

3. How do you face the storms of life? Are you at peace or bristled at the fact you have been called to go through it?

_____

_____

CHAPTER 10
BE STILL AND KNOW

I love the way Isaiah the prophet says it: "You have been a refuge for the poor, a refuge for the needy in his distress, a shelter from the storm and a shade from the heat. For the breath of the ruthless is like a storm driving against a wall" (Isa. 25:4 NIV).

After the storm

I had a dear sister in Christ take me by surprise when she asked what I had learned from going through something unjust. I have been thinking about that question and I want to share my answer. When I was working at the university as the interpreter coordinator, I was easily working sixty hours a week, sometimes more because they gave me a laptop so I could work at home after hours. I also had a second job ten to twelve hours per week *that was my debt-reduction plan.* I have always been a workaholic. Along with that, I was having migraines all the time. I was going in for massages on my shoulders and arms two or three times a month for pain management. I was eating Tums like crazy. And my brow had a permanent deep furrow like I was angry.

Once I resigned, *almost immediately*, the headaches stopped, massages changed to relaxation, and the furrow in my brow softened. Now my stress level is exceptionally low, and my health is better overall. I am hardly ever sick. Work hours dropped to twenty-five or less just at my *second job*. My income dropped to 50 percent of what I had been making, but with the severance package I paid off my debt. For the first time in my life, I was, we were, debt-free. Now I have a new van and payments, but I am three payments ahead. I can pay all my bills, pay for my fun, and have discretionary income.

I was surely headed for a cliff. The stress alone could have killed me. When I think about how close to the edge I was living, all I can think is, "but for the grace of God."

Be Still and Know

After I resigned, I had time on my hands. It was a God-given opportunity to reprioritize my life and my time. As I leaned on God waiting for His answer, I became teachable for the Holy Spirit. I had time to see and enjoy God's creation. Now, I could not only see sunrises and sunsets, but I could take in the beauty and feel the blessing on my soul. With no sixty hours plus schedule to keep, I was able to take my time reading and studying my Bible. I was able to attend ladies Bible class for the first time in years and engage in those in-depth Bible studies. I got to know my sisters in the church family better.

As I spent more time in the Word and in prayer, God opened my eyes to everything and everyone around me. The time spent in the sheep field became a teaching theatre just for me. Time and time again, I would notice the sheep responses to me as their shepherd, good and bad. God knows I am a visual learner, and working with the sheep gave me the opportunity to hold a mirror to my face. I was able to see me up close and personal in my relationship to Him.

I looked forward to these intimate, one-on-one sessions with my God and my Shepherd. I loved spending time outside with the sheep and my sheepdogs. Watching the interaction between them and each other, I could not help but see the direct application to my life and my walk with my Shepherd. From the beginning, I began to come home and write or journal what God was teaching me in the sheep field. I am afraid for the first time in my life I began to truly meditate on His Word, with the help of the Spirit recalling and finding Scriptures that were applicable to the lessons I was learning. I began to memorize Scripture again.

My Treasure

I weathered the storm with Him by my side, really out in front. Now the rainbows I see definitely have a treasure; not *a pot of gold* but something much more precious. I now have time, real quality time, for Kip, for my daughters, and their families. I had time to spend with Mom before she went home to the LORD. I was able to be there for the birth of my daughter Krystal's babies in Kentucky and Alaska. I get to spend time with my grandkids working sheep.

And for the first time in my life, I began to understand the depth of the love and care of the Shepherd for His sheep. It deepened my relationship with God. I have become a better wife, better mother, and a better grandmother. I have joy and peace all the time. I found my purpose; I am using my gifts to teach and to write. I am so very blessed I have a new/renewed identity as a sheep in God's pasture, saved by grace and loved immensely. It does not get any better than that. GOD IS SO GOOD!

I claim the following verses in Isaiah 55 (NIV):

> So is my word that goes out from my mouth;
> it will not return empty, but will accomplish
> what I desire and achieve the purpose for
> which I sent it. You will go out in joy and be
> led forth in peace; the mountains and hills will
> burst into song before you, and all the trees of
> the field will clap their hands. Instead of the
> thornbush will grow the pine tree, and instead
> of briers the myrtle will grow. This will be for
> the LORD's renown, for an everlasting sign,
> which will not be destroyed (Isaiah 55:11-13).

Dance for Joy

Ever watch a toddler when he or she is happy or
excited, especially if there is music? The toddler's
body begins to sway and dance with glee. I believe
all creatures exhibit that same kind of joy when they
feel free to enjoy the pleasures that surround them.
When the storm is over and the fear is subsided, we
too can dance before the Lord, offering praise and
worship to the God who brought us through, and is
forever and always abiding in us. David shares that
thought in the psalms.

Psalm 30:11 (NIV): "You turned my wailing into **dancing**;
you removed my sackcloth and clothed me with joy." And
Psalm 126:5: "Those who sow with tears will **reap** with
songs of joy" (NIV).

The Master Knows You

In 2016, Junebug somehow contracted a bacterial meningitis. The trainer and I first noticed that Junebug, normally very obedient to commands and whistles, suddenly was looking at me bewildered when I gave her a command. It was clear to me because of her character and her strange response that something was wrong. At first it was suspected she was wormy, because that can interfere with their overall health and affect their performance. After the worm treatment, she still seemed confused by my whistles and commands. This might have gone unnoticed in another dog, but with a working border collie and handler team, the two become very aware of each other and readily recognize uncharacteristic responses. I told the vet she is acting confused and somewhat disoriented. He tested for Lyme disease and a myriad of other things –the blood panel came back normal and still no improvement.

He suggested I see a specialist – I took her to one who looked her over and did a few tests to check the dog's responsiveness to stimuli – all good. I was not satisfied; it was not all good; something was wrong – this dog does not refuse commands and is always keenly focused on her sheep, but not now. The vet decided to do a spinal tap and an MRI to determine what was going on. Then she found it – a rare bacterial meningitis.

LESSON 23

The Master knows you and recognizes even the slightest change in your heart.

Junebug was treated over a course of months, and thankfully, her reactions to commands and the keen focus returned. However, now she seemed to be having trouble hearing. The vet felt it would return over time—it did not. How do you tell a dog that the purpose she was made for is no longer an option, that she needs to retire and just be a pet? The answer is you don't. Oh, I tried but regardless of whether she could hear or not, she just wanted to work. So, I continued to take her with me for farm-sitting and practice sessions with sheep. Junebug showed me that while she could not hear, she still knew how to read the sheep and knew how to figure out what I wanted and worked to help me get the job done.

You Know the Master

She is no longer able to compete because she cannot hear the whistles or commands, nor can she follow the signals of the crook when she has her back to me. But regardless of her handicap, she remains useful because she will not accept retirement – she's not a pet; she is a faithful servant to the master.

LESSON 24

Your relationship with the Master is so intimate, you know what the Master wants and strive to help.

About a year later, I was farm-sitting for someone with close to 100 sheep and a place with a lot of acreage. Their neighbor bought some young pigmy goats and penned them next to the adjoining fence under a shade tree. Well, their tree had branches hanging over the sheep farm and the goats decided to take a field trip. I got a call that the neighbor was looking for her goats and if I found them, please take them home. When I went out to gather the sheep, I had both Rascal and Junebug at my side. Junebug was scanning the field, looking for the sheep, and Rascal was playfully running alongside. Junebug saw the sheep first. I sent Rascal because they were some distance and I needed to be able to control the movement. As Rascal brought the sheep to me, I saw the wayward goats in the mix. I had my stick with me and started trying to get the goats separated to one side.

Junebug saw what I was doing, and she took over. As we neared the gate for the sheep pen, Rascal raced up behind and buzzed the sheep, which sent not only the sheep but one of the goats scurrying through the gate. Junebug turned and looked at Rascal with a stern, "Now look what you've done!" look. Then she went in with the other goats and brought them all out together. As I turned to head to the goat neighbor, a friend with me said, "Look at Junebug." I didn't have to; I knew she was herding the goats up behind me. I never said a word to her; it was clear she knew the job and was getting it done.

After that, anytime I go farm-sitting and I just need to gather the sheep up to me, to the barnyard or wherever, I send Junebug. She will always bring them to me and loves the opportunity. When she gets to work, she has a prancing trot step as if to say, "I'm a happy girl, did you see me?" Junebug has shown me repeatedly that while she may no longer compete in a trial, she can still do the chores and wants to. She has no desire to retire and sit idle; she was made for a purpose and she will work as long as she is able.

Limited Abilities – Still Willing to Serve

Like most athletes, there comes a time that the body is just not up to the physical rigor of the sport. Dogs that have been retired often experience a longing and desire to continue serving. No matter how great a dog he or she was, the dog can no longer serve the master like he or she once did. Either they are too slow to catch the sheep or they suffer from arthritis or other ailments. The dogs don't seem to understand why they are no longer called on to serve. Some trainers use retired dogs to start training with young dogs, but the work is so strenuous and they must be able to hear. Now the pleasure of working sheep and serving is reduced to watching sheep and other dogs working from afar.

My dogs are older now: Junebug is thirteen, Tux is eleven, and Rascal is already nine. However, as long as Junebug and Rascal are able and willing, we will continue to herd sheep together.

I am thankful that in the kingdom of God, we can serve as long as we have breath. Our service may change, but we are still very useful in mentoring young Christians as well as other ministries. I love the fact that there is not a time that we are exempt from service or unneeded. God can, and will, always use us if we continue to be willing to work.

As far as a place of honor, that is waiting for us in heaven with our names on it. We are never displaced by a younger servant; our service simply changes until He calls us home.

A Dog's Life

Dogs live in the moment and they enjoy simple pleasures: fetching a ball or a stick, a romp with others, or hanging out together. Many border collies love playing with children and a good game of chase. They take the time to stop and smell the roses, along with everything else in God's creation. They love life best if they serve a purpose. Everyone needs a job to feel useful and satisfied. They work hard and they play hard. They enjoy a good nap next to the master.

We too need to enjoy the simple pleasures that God provides. We need to live our lives in the moment; not weighed down by the past or chasing the future but right where God has us, right now. Life is good and heaven will be even better. Unlike the dogs, we get much more than crumbs from the Master's table. Embrace the daily blessings that God pours into our lives.

LESSON 25

Live in the <u>moment</u>; enjoy <u>simple</u> pleasures.

Sweet Rest for the Weary

No matter the struggle to climb the mountain or the difficulties you face, God is there. Solomon said it best:

> Then you will go on your way in safety, and your foot will not stumble; when you lie down, you will not be afraid; when you lie down, your sleep will be sweet. Have no fear of sudden disaster or of the ruin that overtakes the wicked, for the LORD will be your confidence and will keep your foot from being snared (Proverbs 3:23-26 NIV).

Come take your place at the Master's side, serve the Shepherd.

Questions to Ponder

1. What have you learned from experiencing hardship and injustice? How did God turn your sorrow into joy? List the blessings He has provided.

   _____

   _____

2. Read John 17:6-8, 25-26. How deep is your relationship with the Master? Do you know Him like He knows you?

   _____

   _____

3. Has your service to the Lord changed over time? Do you still feel useful to the Master?

   _____

   _____

4. Are you able to live in the moment? If so, what simple pleasures do you enjoy? If not, pray for clarity that you can see what you are responsible for and, more importantly, what should be left to God alone.

   _____

   _____

LESSONS FROM MY SHEEPDOGS

LESSON 1

Be obedient to the Master, live to serve.

LESSON 2

You cannot manipulate change in others; it will diminish their gifts. Change must come from the desire within.

LESSON 3

Nothing is sweeter than fulfilling God's purpose in your life. He is always calling you to the work and to Him.

LESSON 4

Learn patience and self-control so you can persevere.

LESSON 5

Fix your eyes on the Master. Focus on the lost sheep He sent you to bring home.

LESSON 6

Be ready when the Master calls and give it all you've got.

LESSON 7

"Faith is my personal, positive response to the Word of God, to the point where I act in quiet trust." Phillip Keller, *Lessons From a Sheep Dog A True Story of Transforming Love.*

LESSON 8

That'll Do: **Stop** what you are doing, **return** to the Master, **rest** is waiting.

LESSON 9

You are equipped for the work the Master calls you to.

LESSON 10

Respect the boundaries God has set for you. Be wise with the freedom He allows.

LESSON 11

The need for service does not disappear when you fail to notice.

LESSON 12

If you do not step out of your comfort zone, you are doomed to live a life with no purpose and no fulfillment.

LESSON 13

If you will not focus on the lost, how can the Master use you?

LESSON 14

Obedience is not optional. It is a prerequisite to God's promise, rest, and protection.

LESSON 15

There is no substitute for obedience and no greater delight than to submit to the Master's will – if you know the Master.

LESSON 16

The Shepherd is big enough to aid you in the task and He goes before you.

LESSON 17

The Master always knows and provides what you need.

LESSON 18

The Master is always available and present.

LESSON 19

The first call is a test; the next is to service.

LESSON 20

The Spirit of God works to help you develop anti-venom to ward off the toxic effects of Satan's attacks for those who believe.

LESSON 21

When you do not understand what the Master is doing or why, submit to His will; He will make your paths straight.

LESSON 22

Answer the call no matter what. The Master is waiting. This too shall pass.

LESSON 23

The Master knows you and recognizes even the slightest change in your heart.

LESSON 24

Your relationship with the Master is so intimate, you know what the Master wants and strive to help.

LESSON 25

Live in the moment; enjoy simple pleasures.

Photo by Beth Edwards Photography

GLOSSARY

AKC – The American Kennel Club

ABCA – The American Border Collie Association. The American organization that provides registration certificates and genealogy records for herding border collies.

Crook – Shepherd staff generally measures the length of a walking cane.

Cross Drive – A distance across the width of the trial field. The dog is to drive the sheep calmly across the field in a straight line and move them through the panels on the other side of the field.

Drive – The dog is to push the sheep away from the shepherd or the handler's post in a straight line and move the sheep through the panels for an SDT.

"Eye" – A focused stare at individual sheep or the flock that indicates "I mean business."

Fetch – The dog brings the sheep from the set-out point to the handler at the post or to the shepherd.

Flank – An arc made by the dog around the sheep, either clockwise or counterclockwise.

Grip or Gripping – That is biting the sheep with no provocation. Results in disqualification in an SDT.

Handler – Sheepherding dog owner that uses a set of commands or whistles to direct the dog in gathering and driving sheep on a course for competition or to do chores on the sheep farm.

Hard dog – A dog that takes pressure more easily, but may have a stubborn will.

"Head" – Dog must get out in front and face the sheep (head to head) while exuding confidence.

Lift – When the dog moves the sheep from the position, they were set out at the top of the field.

Outrun – The dog leaves the handler at the post and runs out to gather the sheep in a wide arc until it comes in behind the sheep to move them.

Pen – A pen is set up on the course on either side of the post, at a distance from the post. The handler will open the gate and hold onto a rope on the end of the gate. Together, the dog and the handler move the sheep into the pen and the handler closes the gate.

The Post – Starting point of the dog's run, in competition; it is where the handler stands throughout the run until the sheep are to be penned or shed.

Run — A dog's turn to compete in the sheep dog trial.

Shed – The handler and the dog working together to separate out sheep from the group and hold them separate to take care of the sheep, or until the judge acknowledges the shed in an SDT.

SDT – Sheep Dog Trials. Herding dog competition moving sheep through a preset course. Winning or placing results in points, which qualify the dog for subsequent competitions and cash prizes.

Soft dog – A dog that shies away from pressure, often lacks confidence.

Stock stick – A flexible, heavy-duty plastic stick used to lead or move the sheep.

Whistles – A set of high-pitched tones matched with specific commands for the sheepdog to follow when at a distance from the shepherd or handler.

BIBLIOGRAPHY

"Border Collie History: From Old Hemp to New Beginnings." Accessed April 18, 2021. ColliePoint.com. https://colliepoint.com/border-collie-history.

BC Museum: "AULDHEMP." Last modified July 15, 2013. Accessed April 18, 2021. www.bordercolliemuseum.org.

Fritz, Julie."Border Collie A Smart and High Energy Breed." Last updated February 16, 2021. Accessed August 11, 2021. https//www.caninejournal.com/border-collie.

Jeng, Richard. ""Are Border Collies Smart? – Here's Why They're the Smartest." Published July 7, 2021. Accessed August 11, 2021. thesmartcanine.com.

Keller, Philip. *Lessons From a Sheep Dog A True Story of Transforming Love.* Nashville, Tennessee. Thomas Nelson. Reprint edition September 2002.

McCaig, Donald. *The Dog Wars How the Border Collie Battled the American Kennel Club.* Hillsborough, New Jersey. Outrun Press. 2007.

O'Brien, Christine. "Best Farm Dogs for Life in the Country." Published August 20, 2018. Accessed August 16, 2021. https://www.hillspet.com/dog-care/ new-pet-parent/ best-farm-dog-breeds.

"Old Hemp Grandfather of Border Collies." Posted December 9, 2015. Last updated 2021. Accessed April 18, 2021. https://guildofshepherdsandcollies.com/old-hemp-grandfather -of -the -border collie.

PetBlog. "10 Best Sheep Herding Dog Breeds" Last Updated April 2, 2021. Accessed August 16, 2021. https://petblog.org/sheep-herding-dogs/.

Phips, Whitney. "If the mountain were smooth, you couldn't climb it." Published June 2013. Accessed January 1, 2021. Elephant Journal. https://www.elephantjournal.com "If The Mountain Were Smooth, You Couldn't Climb It." {Wintley Phipps} | elephantjournal.

"The 25 Most Obedient Mid-Size Dog Breeds" Newsweek. Published February 27, 2021. Accessed August 13, 2021. https://www.newsweek.com/best-dogs-mid-size-obedient-breeds-1572326.

"These Are the Most Obedient Dog Breeds." Newsweek. Published November 30, 2020. Accessed August 13, 2021. https://www.newsweek.com/here-are-most-obedient-dog-breeds-1551213

William. "What are the Smartest Dog Breeds 2021." Last updated June 17, 2021. Accessed August 11, 2021. https://collieslife.com.

CPSIA information can be obtained
at www.ICGtesting.com
Printed in the USA
BVHW051626231121
622347BV00020B/919